In
the
Beginning:

Genesis People Speak

★ ★ ★

Jana Carman

ISBN-13: 978-1537608860 (CreateSpace-Assigned)
ISBN-10: 153760886X

In Appreciation

To John, my beloved husband of many years, for his love and encouragement in using my gifts— all my love and gratitude.

To my loving family: thoughtful Mary with her expanding tribe, Tom with his delightful sense of humor, Ruth the multi-gifted, Kate who amazes me with her personal courage and generosity, and the children and others they have added to our family—thank you all!

To my sister, Pan Sankey, proofreader extraordinaire who always makes me look good—without a doubt because she is such a good writer herself—my deepest appreciation. I'm glad we're sisters!

My parents, now in glory, gave me a foundation in Scripture, a delight in books and music, and ten years of piano lessons plus four of college—who could ask for more! They launched me into the worlds of music, living for God, and serving others. I am forever grateful.

Contents

Numbers following Chapter Titles indicate chapters in Genesis

The following poems by Betty Spence
are included with her gracious permission:
Coming of Age
Enoch's Crossing
Window of Hope
Overheard in the Upper Room
The Devotion of Laughter
Peniel
So This is Where

All other poems and narratives
by Jana Carman

"God meant it for good."

Preface

These narratives and poems are like houses. Scripture forms the foundation but, as in houses, what is built on the foundation varies greatly according to the architect's imagination. Some of these narratives rely heavily on the foundation and combine many experiences. Others, based on a single incident, are constructed from what someone called "sanctified imagination," –it could have happened and, to the best of my ability, it doesn't contradict scripture.

I try to get inside the person's skin, to feel his or her experience. After all, these Genesis people were not cardboard stand-ups, they were real flesh and blood people. They loved, they hated, they hurt, they hurt others, they walked with God, they fell into sin. People whose lives are examples of what to do and what not to do—just like us. Who knows? You may find yourself in these pages.

I hope these narratives and poems will help you look with new eyes at the Bible, its stories, its real people, its principles, its Author.

Chapter 1. In the Beginning

In the beginning God created the heavens and the earth. Now the earth was formless and empty, darkness was over the surface of the deep, and the Spirit of God was hovering over the waters. And God said: "Let there be . . . .

CREATION MUSIC

When triune God sang, "Let there be . . . ,"
their three rich notes formed a chord,
and complex, glorious harmony
vibrated like a kettledrum
(called by some "Big Bang") and spun
into existence building blocks
    of all that is,
    all that will be.
Sometimes we catch the echo
of that song and strain to hear
the thrum of God-sung harmonies,
the whisper of the whirling spheres.
In concert, someday, at the Throne,
we'll hear those pure, sweet, thrilling tones
    that once composed
    the world's first song.

And God said: "Let there be light," and there was light . . . "
And God said: "Let there be a vault between the waters . . . "
And God said, "Let the water under the sky be gathered into one place, and let dry land appear . . . "
Then God said, "Let the land produce vegetation . . . "
And God said, "Let there be lights in the vault of the sky . . . "
And God said, "Let the water teem with living creatures and let birds fly above the earth across the vault of the sky . . ."
And God said, "Let the land produce living creatures according to their kinds."
Then God said, "Let us make mankind in our image, in our likeness . . . "
God saw all that he had made, and it was very good.
(Genesis 1:1,2,3,6,11,14,20,24,26,31)

In the beginning was the Word, and the Word was with God, and the Word was God. He was with God in the beginning. Through him all things were made; without him nothing was made that has been made . . . .
The Word became flesh and made his dwelling among us. (John 1:1-3,14)

IN THE BEGINNING

A mighty Word was spoken,
its rolling sound evoking
into being everything.
Echoes will reverberate
along the corridors of time
and even through eternity,
telling of God's consummate
verbal creativity.

Thus the heavens and the earth were completed in all their vast array. By the seventh day God had finished the work he had been doing; so on the seventh day he rested from all his work. Then God blessed the seventh day and made it holy, because in it he rested from all the work of creating he had done.
(Genesis 2:1-3)

After the busiest week ever, God rested. Then, he planted a garden, the most beautiful and fruitful place anyone could imagine. But there was no one to care for this garden, and everyone knows what happens to untended gardens.

So, God made a gardener—and a helper.

EARTH DAY

God took a handful of nothing
and made something.
He took a handful of something
and made someone.
He took a handful from someone
and made another someone,
like, yet different.

Then God told our parents—
made from nothing made from
something made from someone—
that Earth was theirs (and ours) to tend.
From earth we came,
by earth's bounty we are sustained,
to earth we shall return.

And, as God Himself once judged,
everything He made was
Very Good.

So the LORD God caused the man to fall into a deep sleep; and while he was sleeping, he took one of the man's ribs and then closed up the place with flesh. Then the LORD God made a woman from the rib he had taken out of the man, and he brought her to the man. The man said, "This is now bone of my bones and flesh of my flesh; she shall be called 'woman,' for she was taken out of man." That is why a man leaves his father and mother and is united to his wife, and they become one flesh. (Genesis 2:21-24)

DAY IN THE GARDEN

Morning.
From strings of dewdrops,
spears of light struck tiny rainbows—
promising another day
of joy and fellowship.

Noon.
Their pleasant morning's work complete,
as healthy hunger stirred within,
the two walked hand in hand
toward the garden's heart.

*And the LORD God commanded the man, "You are free to eat from any tree in the garden, but **you must not eat from the tree of the knowledge of good and evil,** for when you eat from it you will certainly die."...*
Now the serpent ... said to the woman, "Did God really say, 'You must not eat from any tree in the garden'? ... You will not certainly die. ... For God knows that when you eat from it your eyes will be opened, and you will be like God, knowing good and evil." ... She took some and ate it. She also gave some to her husband, who was with her, and he ate it. ... (Genesis 2:16,17; 3:1,4,6)

"You will be like God, knowing good and evil." The sly serpent tells enough truth to make a course of action reasonable, but always, always, there lurks the hidden lie. They learned. Oh, what painful lessons they learned!

They learned the fruit of disobedience was delicious—for the moment.

They learned that they were naked.

They learned about fear where there had been only fellowship with God.

They learned the ploy of pass the blame. "It was her fault; well, really, God, it's Your fault because You gave her to me." "Actually, it was the serpent's fault. He deceived me."

(Unfortunately they did not learn to ignore the tempter; nor do we.)

But the most painful lesson—they learned that disobedience has consequences.

Terrible consequences. Painful childbirth. Submission to another. Dealing with a ground cursed to produce thorns and thistles. Unending hard work just to raise enough to eat. And – death.

[You will] *return to the ground, since from it you were taken;*
for dust you are and to dust you will return. (Genesis 3:19)

Evening.
Such pain! All from that fruit,
delectable to tongue, deadly to the soul.
Ashamed, estranged, now driven out.
A flashing sword bars the garden's gate.

So the LORD God banished him from the Garden of Eden to work the ground
from which he had been taken. After he drove the man out, he placed on the
east side of the Garden of Eden cherubim and a flaming sword flashing back
and forth to guard the way to the tree of life.   (Genesis 3:23,24)

AFTER THE APPLE

God said, They are now as we—
knowing all, all bad, all good—
because they ate from that one tree,
the one banned tree in Eden's wood.
    As innocents, they knew well
    all that's wholesome, happy, chaste.
    But now, sin taints each good with hell,
    each sweet with bitter after-taste.
With fatal knowledge the result
of that first tree—should they partake
from the second, what could halt
deathlessness—far worse mistake!
    Immortals driven mad by hate,
    betrayals, nightmare without end,
    enmeshed within a cruel fate,
    trapped in distrust, disease – condemned
to unabating pain, to lust
devoid of love, to drawing breath
for endless, joyless eons, must
be life without the hope of death.

I love too much, the Father said,
to let that happen. Greater love
demands their exile. Satan's head
will yet be bruised, sin's taint removed.
Without temptation of that tree,
my children may come home to Me.

COMING OF AGE

by Betty Spence

Driven
from that verdant,
 virgin land
we are bereft.
No longer
artless children
unaware
of time and passing,
we must make for ourselves
gardens whose trees,
paths and fountains
give us pause.
Knowing
we might have obeyed—
(unable to un-know)
and might have
chosen innocence
over encounter,
we must live
with the knowledge
that words other than
in the mouth of God
may not mean
what they seem.

* * *

FIXING THE BLAME

Adam: It's all your fault! If you hadn't spoiled him, Eve—

Eve: I! Adam, how can you say that? Who was so proud of his firstborn son? Who bragged how Cain could make anything grow despite the curse on the ground?

Adam: Of course I was proud. But you can't deny you encouraged him to bring you all the things he had grown.

Eve: Well, of course. They were delicious, and we had to eat. So why is it all my fault? You ate his vegetables too, you know.

Adam: But you complained I was being cruel when I tried to correct him. "God gave us free will," you said.

Eve: How soon I forgot that *our* free will, misused, had brought us banishment . . . .

Adam: And if ever a child needed correcting, it was Cain.

Eve: Such a temper he had, always wanting his own way, rebellious, so sure he was right ....

Adam: Yes, and everyone else was wrong! While Abel was the opposite—gentle, easy-going,

Eve: obedient and trusting.

Adam: *Too* trusting, of his brother, anyway.

Eve: But who would ever guess that Cain would hate enough to kill?

Adam: Two sons, so different—

Eve: and now both are gone. Oh Adam, where did we go wrong?

Adam: It's hard to raise children when you were never a child yourself.

Eve: We've made some awful mistakes.

Adam: And our failure with Cain was not the first.

Eve: *Don't* bring that up again, Adam. You ate it too.

Adam: Now, Eve, did I mention—

Eve: You didn't have to. It's always there, behind every argument.

Adam: How innocent we were. We never dreamed just how damning the knowledge of evil could be. First we lost Eden,

Eve: now we've lost both sons,

Adam: one dead,

Eve: one banished.

Adam: Yet we, the original sinners remain,

Eve: seeing sin's dreadful fruit,

Adam: feeling pain heaped on pain.

Eve: I'm sometimes strangely drawn to that gate, closed to us now and guarded. I linger there, wishing . . .

Adam: Wishing—yes, I know. Me too. Wishing we could go back,

Eve: yet knowing we never can.

Adam: Remember how it felt, walking and talking with God in the cool of each evening?

Eve: Remember how it felt, that holy joy, that oneness, that friendship?

Adam: I think that's what I miss the most.

Eve: We could talk to Him about anything! Oh, if only –

Adam: Yes, if only everything could be as it was before!

Eve: No mountain of guilt weighing down my soul.

Adam: No alienation from God,

Both: and from each other.

Adam: But now, when our problems are unfixable,

Eve: we just tend to –to fix the blame. It's all my fault.

If only I hadn't listened . . .

Adam: No, my fault. If only I had stopped you . . . .

Both: If only . . . .

* * *

Chapter 2. In His Own Likeness

ADAM'S LINE

When God created mankind, he made them in the likeness of God. He created them male and female and blessed them.

When Adam had lived 130 years, he had a son in his own likeness, in his own image, and he named him Seth. After Seth was born, Adam lived 800 years and had other sons and daughters. Altogether Adam lived a total of 930 years, and then he died.

When Seth had lived 150 years, he became the father of Enosh. ... After Enosh [was born], Seth lived 807 years and had other sons and daughters. Altogether Seth lived a total of 912 years.

When Enosh had lived 90 years, he became the father of Kenan. ... After Kenan [was born], Enosh lived 815 years and had other sons and daughters. Altogether, Enosh lived ... 905 years.

* * *

BEFORE – AND AFTER

Kenan, Adam's great-grandson:

"Great-grandpa Adam, can I ask you something?"

"Of course, boy. Now which one are you? You're not Seth's boy, are you? I'm sure he would be older than you. You must be Enosh."

"No, Great-grandpa Adam, Enosh is my father. I'm Kenan."

"Oh yes, Seth and then Enosh, and now you. My, how time flies. I must be almost four hundred years old now. But, yes, Kenan. What do you want to know?"

"What was it like "before"?"

"Before? What do you mean?"

"I mean, before you and Great-grandmother Eve had to move?"

"Oh. *That* Before. Yes, yes. Well, I don't know if I can explain it so you can understand, because it was so different, not at all like now. But I will try. Is there any special thing you're curious about?"

"Tell me about the first time you woke up."

"Well, it's hard to explain, it's almost like being a brand new baby, and learning about the world around you. But the first thing I felt was – I was – Other."

"I don't know what you mean, Great-grandfather."

"It's hard to put into words. Try this: are you exactly the same as your brother? Or are you different?"

"We're not the same, even though we have the same parents. And we have a sister too, and she looks almost like us, but she is another of our family."

"Yes, an Other. So you and your brother and sister are Others, each different from each Other."

"Yeah, I guess so. But who else was there, so you felt like an Other?"

"My Father-Creator was there, right beside me, but He was so, so very – well, different from me, from all around me, and I knew He had made me, yet He was so infinitely Other. And I soon found out that I too was Other. I was Other than the animals. I had skin and they had fur—most of them.

"And when I looked around, I saw that I was Other than growing things, like trees and plants. We both were living, yet I could move and they were planted and remained in one place."

"What else seemed strange or different?"

"I remember a breeze brushed against my skin, and I felt it but couldn't touch it or see it, even when the leaves moved, so I knew there were Other things that were real but I couldn't see them. And then, after a while, well – Tell me, Kenan, how do you know you are hungry?"

"I just know it. Sometimes my stomach growls, and I know what that means."

"But if you had never had felt it before, how would you know?"

"Maybe—like babies? Babies don't really *know* they are hungry, but they cry."

"Yes, that's right, they do, Kenan. And that was something like I felt. I wanted to eat, even though I had never eaten before nor felt hungry, but God had made me so that somehow I knew I needed both food and water."

"That's funny, Great-grandpa. You were really like a baby."

"Yes, God had given me instincts, those purely physical ones, but other instincts too. As far as we can tell, newborn babies seem to need more than just milk, they need to be cuddled. Although I was not a baby but a full-sized man, I felt a need for closeness, for companion-ship. For a while God and I had wonderful walks and talks. That was one of the things I missed most, After.

"But, back to Before. That first day was a day of many First Times, many discoveries. When it started to get dark, I was startled. I didn't know what darkness or night was. Where did the light go and would it ever come back? I hesitated to close my eyes, but I was tired and I fell asleep—that was a First Time too—and when I woke up I was glad to see that the light had returned. When it started to get dark again, I was not so afraid since I had already experienced the return of the sun."

"How long were you alone?"

"Oh, I wasn't alone. I had my animal friends, and best of all, I had Father God's constant presence, assurance that he was my friend, even though I couldn't see him. That is one of the worse things about –After. I no longer felt his presence, his companionship, and if you have once known that, its absence is unbearably hard.

"But you had Great-grandmother Eve then, didn't you?"

"Yes, and it helped, but it wasn't the same. Couldn't be. But I suppose you want to hear about Eve, don't you? Most people are interested in that. In some ways it was very like when I first "woke" to knowing I was alive."

"Was it like babies being born now?"

"No, I assure you, it was not at all like the way babies are born, now. Now we know a baby is coming because the mother's body changes. For me, there was no advance notice. I just woke up and there she was. Father-God told me that He had fashioned her from part of me, so what had been one was now two. And most definitely, not two the same. The differences were very appealing, we each agreed.

"But Eve was flesh of my flesh and heart of my heart, and we immediately knew that we were One though two. And she loved Father-God as I did. We would walk together with Him in the evenings after our day's work was done. Those were such beautiful times. Even now, hundreds of years later, my heart yearns for those times when our hearts —Eve's, mine and God's —were filled with pure love and delight in each other's company.

Oh, Father-God, I miss You so! Will I ever walk in the Garden with You again?"

"I'm sorry, Great-grandpa Adam, I didn't mean to make you sad by my questions."

"That's all right, young Kenan. Sadness, like thorns, is part of our punishment. From our disobedience, sin spread like weeds, like poison. Evil is in us and all around us. I fear that God will lose patience with our wickedness. If a holy God should regret that He made us, He will bring on us unimaginable disaster, and we will deserve it. Ah yes, we will indeed deserve it!

"Young Kenan, make sure that you keep the knowledge of our great Father-God alive in your heart. That is the only hope for our race."

"Great-grandpa, I hear my mother calling, so I'd better run and do my chores. Thank you for telling me about Before."

"Yes, run along, young Kenan. But keep in mind *my* After. God loves us, but like a good father, He will not forever withhold His hand. Make sure to tell your children and children's children. They need to know that. Father-God loves, but He does not overlook disobedience. I know. Oh, how I know!"   *(Kenan & Adam)*

* * *

And so Adam's line extended: Kenan to Mahalel, to Jared, to Enoch, to Methuselah. But there is a break in the usual format.

"When Enoch had lived 65 years, he became the father of Methuselah. After he became the father of Methuselah, Enoch walked faithfully with God 300 years. … Then he was no more, because God took him away."   (Genesis 5:22-24)

ENOCH'S CROSSING
by Betty Spence

In step
with God, Enoch
never knew when the road

an out and the bridge of faith locked
in place.

Walked with God. Walked *faithfully* with God.

In all those centuries since Adam and Eve walked with God in the Garden, here was the first mention of someone else who walked with God. (Adam's lifespan, given as 930 years, indicates that he was still around in Enoch's time and died during Methuselah's lifetime.)

When Methuselah had lived 187 years, he became the father of Lamech. ... After Lamech..., Methuselah lived 782 years and had other sons and daughters. Altogether Methuselah lived 969 years, and then he died.

When Lamech had lived 182 years, he had a son. He named him Noah [which sounds like 'comfort'] and said, "He will comfort us in the labor and painful toil of our hands caused by the ground the LORD has cursed." After Noah was born, Lamech lived 595 years and had other sons and daughters. Altogether Lamech lived 777 years, and then he died.

After Noah was 500 years old, he became the father of Shem, Ham and Japheth. (Genesis 5)

So now onto the stage of history comes Noah, the third man who walked with God. *(Genesis 6:9)*

When God looks for someone to do a big job, these are the qualities God looks for:
1. "Noah found favor in the eyes of the Lord. "
2. "Noah was a righteous man,
3. "blameless among the people of his time."
4. "He walked faithfully with God."
5. "Noah did everything just as God commanded him."
    (Genesis 6:8,9,22)

* * *

Chapter 3. The Great Flood

BUT WHY KILL EVERYBODY?

The LORD saw how great the wickedness of the human race had become on the earth, and that every inclination of the thoughts of the human heart was only evil all the time. The LORD regretted that he had made human beings on the earth, and his heart was deeply troubled.

So the LORD said, "I will wipe from the face of the earth the human race I have created—and with them the animals, the birds and the creatures that move along the ground —for I regret that I have made them."

But Noah found favor in the eyes of the LORD.   *(Genesis 6:5-8)*

* * *

THE FLOATING ZOO

Mrs. Noah:

I was one who never liked animals in the house! "Leave the cat outside, Noah," I would say. "That's why God gave her a fur coat."

So when my husband told me he was building a floating zoo in our back yard, and **why**, I said, "Not me, Noah. I don't do zoos. You'll have to find another cook for that ocean voyage."

And he said, "You'll get used to the idea. Especially when the choice is that or swimming."

Well, I had time to get used to the idea, because there was a stretch of a hundred years between God giving Noah the blueprints and those first raindrops. It might have been shorter if Noah hadn't knocked off work so often to preach to the neighbors. Not that they listened. They thought he was crazy. So did I, sometimes.

Do you know what it's like having an unfinished building project in the back yard for a *hundred years*? And of course you can't hide something that big. People came from miles around to gawk and laugh. So down went the tools while Noah explained that God ("Who is God?" they'd ask) was going to send a flood ("What's a flood?") that would drown the whole world. They would double up with laughter and go away twirling their fingers beside their heads.

My boys got pressed into helping their father build this monstrosity. They were excited to be able to help Daddy at first, but after the first forty years or so, they got a bit tired of felling trees, sawing and pounding nails. However, towards the end there was other work such as storing hay and feed in the holds, so they could trade off jobs.

Our neighbors gave us a rough time. They had no patience with Noah and his preaching, or his backyard project. Because so many came to gawk at the ark, they complained that he was building an "attractive nuisance" (whatever that is). They came around to jeer and throw stones when we were worshipping. In fact, other than our small family—Noah and me, our three boys and their wives— nobody else still worshipped the true God. Well, I guess Methuselah did, come to think of it. He was Noah's grandfather. He died just before the rains started. Noah said he was 969 years old. Longevity certainly runs in his family. Noah himself is 600 years old. My age? Don't ask.

The Lord then said to Noah, "Go into the ark, you and your whole family, because I have found you righteous in this generation. ... And Noah and his sons and his wife and his sons' wives entered the ark to escape the waters of the flood. (Genesis 7:1,7)

Well, anyway, the animals arrived and it seemed like the floodgates of heaven were opened. Noah hurried all of us into the boat, and then God himself shut the door. Soon even all the noise the animals made couldn't drown out the cries and pounding on the outside. "Can't we let some in?" I begged Noah. "My mother? My sister's baby boy?"

But he shook his head sadly. "God shut the door, Tirzah, and I can't open it. They had their chance and didn't take it." After a while

I was glad that we couldn't hear any more voices. It had torn my heart in two, thinking I recognized certain voices outside.

For forty days the flood kept coming on the earth, and as the waters increased they lifted the ark high above the earth. ... Every living thing on the face of the earth was wiped out; people and animals and the creatures that move along the ground and the birds were wiped out. Only Noah was left, and those with him in the ark.   *(Genesis 7:17,23)*

PRAYER OF A MOLE ON THE ARK

Lord,
  I am homesick for dirt, for tender grubs.
  I hide in dark corners of this huge boat,
 but it's not the same--my eyes hurt,
 and I fear the openness, the prowling cats.
It's been so long, Lord. A year to me
  is like two hundred years to Noah.
Will I ever tunnel in my native earth again before I die?
And if I won't, does heaven have a patch somewhere
  of rich dark dirt where humble moles
  can dig to heart's content? If so,
    I'll gladly say Amen.

* * *

Life fell into a routine. The men and the boys' wives, as well, were kept busy feeding the animals and mucking out, as they called it. We got used to the animal smell and to the constant motion of the ark. So when the ark ground against a mountaintop, I couldn't figure out at first what was happening.

* * *

The water receded steadily from the earth. At the end of the hundred and fifty days the water had gone down, and on the seventeenth day of the seventh month the ark came to rest on the mountains of Ararat. The waters continued to recede until the tenth month, and on the first day of the tenth month the tops of the mountains became visible.
After forty days Noah opened a window he had made in the ark and sent out a raven, and it kept flying back and forth until the water had dried up from the earth. Then he sent out a dove to see if the water had receded from the surface

of the ground. But the dove could find nowhere to perch … so it returned to Noah in the ark. … He waited seven more days and again sent out the dove from the ark. When the dove returned to him in the evening, there in its beak was a freshly plucked olive leaf! … He waited seven more days and sent the dove out again, but this time it did not return to him. (Genesis 8:3-12)

* * *

WINDOW OF HOPE
by Betty Spence

O Lord, this ark of mine and Noah's rides
  Upon the very floods and rising tides
    Of abandonment
    You have divinely sent
To judge the wicked and the innocent.

And like the patriarch of old, may I
  Now hear the rush of wings and the soft, low cry
    Of a mourning dove
    Bearing from above
A message of God's never-ending love.

While at the window of hope I watch, and wait
  For overwhelming sorrow to abate.
    Lord, may mine be
    The beauty of a tree
That strikes new leaves despite adversity.

* * *

By the first day of the first month of Noah's six hundred and first year, the water had dried up from the earth. … By the twenty-seventh day of the second month the earth was completely dry. Then God said to Noah, "Come out of the ark, you and your wife and your sons and their wives. Bring out every kind of living creature that is with you—the birds, the animals, and all the creatures that move along the ground—so they can multiply on the earth and be fruitful and increase in number on it."   *(Genesis 8:13,14-17)*

But, you know, it's funny. I really didn't want to go into that thing. Now I don't want to come out. It seems safer inside. And outside is so— so terribly empty. It frightens me.

Noah has set up a tent for me. Maybe in a day or so, I can make myself go outside.

But I'll tell you one thing. I'm not having a cat or any other animal, no matter how cute and cuddly, in my new house. There I draw the line! I've had enough animals to last me a lifetime, even if I live to be as old as Noah's grandfather, Methuselah.   (Mrs. Noah)

* * *

GOD'S COVENANT WITH NOAH

Noah:

A whole year in that boat! It's good to have earth under my feet again, even though it still feels like I'm rocking on waves.

First thing, I built an altar for burnt sacrifice using some of the "clean" animals and birds. The LORD was pleased with the sacrifice, and promised:

"Never again will I curse the ground because of humans, even though every inclination of the human heart is evil from childhood. And never again will I destroy all living creatures, as I have done. As long as the earth endures, seedtime and harvest, cold and heat, summer and winter, day and night will never cease."

(Genesis 8:21,22)

* * *

That is a wonderful promise, but it makes me wonder: if mankind gets as bad as it was before when God felt he had to wipe it out, what then? Surely he won't just ignore his creation when it goes so terribly wrong. Does God have another way to cleanse evil hearts? Well, he is God, so I am sure he has a plan.

God blessed us then, telling us that, in addition to green plants, we could eat "everything that lives and moves" just as long as we don't eat anything that still contains blood. He seems to be very concerned about blood.

In addition to God's promise, he made a formal, binding agreement with me and all who would follow me:

I now establish my covenant with you and with your descendants after you, and with every living creature that was with you. ... Never again will all life be destroyed by the waters of a flood; never again will there be a flood to destroy the earth. ... I have set my rainbow in the clouds, and it will be the sign of the covenant between me and the earth. (Genesis 9:8,11,13)

"Never again." God said it three times. Never again. No matter how terribly wrong we become. And we will, I know. Even we who walk with God still have the inner urge to do the wrong thing, the thing that displeases God or hurts others. Yes. Me too.

I'm a man of the soil, so I planted a vineyard. When the grapes ripened, I made wine and got drunk. My son Ham saw me passed out and naked. Thinking it was funny, he told his brothers. Concerned for the respect due their father, they covered me up without looking at me.

When I found out about it, I actually cursed Ham and his descendants to become the slaves of his brother Shem. The tongue is the hardest part of the body to master! Our words have power, especially uttered in anger. Three hundred years later I still remember my sins. Drunk, angry, cursing. O God, forgive me. *(Noah)*

After the flood Noah lived 350 years. Noah lived a total of 950 years, and then he died. (Genesis 9:28,29)

From these [Noah's descendants] the nations spread out over the earth after the flood. (Genesis 10:32b)

* * *

Chapter 4. New Beginnings

BABEL

Now the whole world had one language and a common speech. As men moved eastward, they found a plain in Shinar and settled there. ... Then they said, "Come, let us build ourselves a city, with a tower that reaches to the heavens, so that we may make a name for ourselves. ....

But the LORD came down to see the city and the tower the people were building. The LORD said, "If as one people speaking the same language they have begun to do this, then nothing they plan to do will be impossible for them. Come, let us go down and confuse their language so they will not understand each other.

So the LORD scattered them from there over all the earth, and they stopped building the city. That is why it was called Babel—because there the LORD confused the language of the whole world. *(Genesis 11:1,2,4-9)*

* * *

When the day of Pentecost came, they were all together in one place. Suddenly a sound like the blowing of a violent wind came from heaven and filled the whole house where they were sitting. They saw what seemed to be tongues of fire that separated and came to rest on each of them. All of them were filled with the Holy Spirit and began to speak in other tongues as the Spirit enabled them.

Now there were staying in Jerusalem God-fearing Jews from every nation under heaven. When they heard this sound, a crowd came together in bewilderment, because each one heard them speaking in his own language. *(Acts 2:1-6)*

* * *

OVERHEARD in the UPPER ROOM
by Betty Spence

The wind has changed and never more suddenly . . .
have you ever known it to sound just like this?
Now wind . . . now fire . . . now heavenly fire rained down.
You know —the top of your head is in a blaze . . .
can it be, the tongue of the learned is now mine, too?
Have I, have you, become a burning bush
whose every leaf is a fiery tongue
witnessing to something heard, something seen?
O Holy Ghost and Fire, O Living Flame!
In tongues other than my own, I praise your name.

THE CURSE REVERSED

At Pentecost God reversed
the Babel curse.
No longer "making a name for ourselves"
but unable to understand each other.
At Pentecost God came as flame,
broke down barriers,
helped us speak,
accept, feast together.
He made His Name
a Name for all to hear,
a Name which makes aliens
into family, brothers and sisters
in Christ.

* * *

FROM SHEM TO ABRAM

Two years after the flood, when Shem was 100 years old, he became the father of Arphaxad. And after he became the father of Arphaxad, Shem lived 500 years and had other sons and daughters.
When Arphaxad had lived 35 years, he became the father of Shelah ... [and] lived 403 years and had other sons and daughters.
When Shelah had lived 30 years, he became the father of Eber ... [and] lived 403 years .... (Genesis 11:10-15)

As the line from Noah stretched on, the age of each man when his son was born shrunk from Shem who was 100, to the next generations which averaged 32. Also the long length of years until death shrunk from 600 total (Shem) to 205 (Terah, father of Abram). (If you are interested in the actual figures, read Genesis 11:10-25.)

Since genealogical descent was so important, most of Genesis 11 reports the line from Noah to Abram. In old English style used by the King James Version the line goes like this:

Eber begat Peleg. Peleg begat Reu. Reu begat Serug. Serug begat Nahor. Nahor begat Terah.

After Terah had lived 70 years, he became the father of Abram, Nahor, and Haran. ... Haran became the father of Lot. While his father Terah was still alive, Haran died in Ur of the Chaldeans, in the land of his birth.
Abram and Nahor both married. The name of Abram's wife was Sarai, and the name of Nahor's wife was Milkah; she was the daughter of Haran, the father of both Milkah and Iskah. Now Sarai was childless because she was not able to conceive.
Terah took his son Abram, his grandson Lot the son of Haran, and his daughter-in-law Sarai, the wife of his son Abram, and together they set out from Ur of the Chaldeans to go to Canaan. But when they came to Haran, they settled there.
Terah lived 205 years, and he died in Haran.
(Genesis 11:26-32)

The stage is set, the characters are in place for Abram's family who will fill the rest of the book of Genesis with their all-too-human failures and successes.

God had great plans for Abram's family, plans he never would have believed, had not God himself told him. He was told to leave his home country and go —well, he wasn't told where.

But the LORD had made very special promises to Abram, and Abram believed God would do it.

God said it.

He believed it.

And that's good enough for him!

Chapter 5. Abram's Call

HEADING FOR CANAAN

The LORD had said to Abram, "Leave your country, your people,
  and your father's household and go to the land I will show you.
  I will make you into a great nation and I will bless you;
  and you will be a blessing.
  I will bless those who bless you, and whoever curses you I will curse;
  and all peoples on earth will be blessed through you. (Genesis 12:1-3)

Abram:

I left the country of my birth as the LORD told me. He also said to leave my relatives and my father's family, but my father Terah was well over 100, and as the oldest son I was responsible for his welfare. Also my brother Haran had died, so I felt obligated to take his son Lot with me. I couldn't abandon either of them. And my other brother Nahor and his wife Milcah decided to come along. (I hope God understood why I hadn't done exactly as he told me to do. Or is that the common excuse for not quite obeying?)

With Sarai, my wife, and the others, we traveled west, headed for –well, we didn't know where. God hadn't told me yet. In fact he didn't tell me until I had "left my father's household and people" behind in Haran, several years later.

When we reached the town of Haran (no relation to my dead brother), we stopped. It was a thriving place for caravans to stop. It also was a place of moon-god worship, and because that was the main god back in Ur, my father and brother really felt comfortable. I didn't. My God actually talked to me, unlike their moon-god who seemed as far away as the moon itself.

Nevertheless, we stayed at Haran much longer than we should have, and my brother Nahor decided he wanted to settle there. My father also stayed in Haran until his death at age 205. Yes, except for my brother Haran, we are a long-lived people. Many years later I sent my servant back to Haran to get a bride for Isaac from among my kin. But that's a story for later.

I was about 75 when Sarai, Lot and I finally left Haran, heading south to Canaan. We made quite a caravan with all of our possessions plus the servants we had acquired in Haran. The LORD had told me, "Go to the land I will show you." No map. No name to ask for. Just—go. But—and this may sound a bit presumptuous—my God was my friend, and I was his friend. You trust your friend because you know your friend loves you and has your best interests in mind. I trusted him.

The LORD had made me a promise. I believed him. He said, "I will make your name great, and you will be a blessing. I will bless those who bless you, and whoever curses you I will curse; and all peoples on earth will be blessed through you." With a promise like that, anyone should be willing to step out, even without knowing where to go. It's not that I possessed a great and unusual faith. It's just that I had confidence in a great God—unlike that moon-god my people worshiped.

As we traveled southward, entering Canaan, I waited for God's indication, hoping for an inner assurance that this place is the right place. The assurance did not come, so we continued down to Shechem, and the great tree of Moreh where the Canaanites worshiped their gods.

While we camped there, the LORD appeared to me again. He made another promise to me, saying, "To your offspring I will give this land." I built an altar there to the LORD and worshiped him.

But I had no feeling of this being home, so I moved on, building another altar between Bethel and Ai, before continuing toward the Negev.

* * *

"SHE'S MY SISTER"

The land was experiencing a famine—not the first and unlikely to be the last—so I decided to go to Egypt where food was usually more available.

Now I must tell you that my wife Sarai was a most beautiful woman. Everywhere we went men's eyes were drawn to her. I was told that there were whispers that she would be a great prize if her husband could be eliminated.

As we were entering Egypt, I seriously feared that someone would kill me in order to get her. I asked her to say she was my sister and then I would be treated well. Well, it was almost true because she *was* my sister—half-sister actually since she was my father's daughter but by a different mother.

The ruse worked for a bit, until Pharaoh's officials saw her, praised her to Pharaoh, and she was taken into his palace. Being Sarai's "brother not husband" was quite profitable for me: I acquired sheep, cattle, male and female donkeys, male and female servants and camels. But serious problems—diseases—arose in Pharaoh's household. When Pharaoh found out that having Sarai in his house was the cause, and that she was actually my wife, he –well, he could have had me killed, but instead he said, "Take your wife and get out of here." And he made sure that my wife and I and all our possessions were sent on our way, out of his country.

It's embarrassing, being kicked out of a country, but at least we were still alive. We made our way up to the Negev, and eventually back to the place between Bethel and Ai where I had first built an altar. And that's where trouble erupted between Lot's herdsmen and mine.

Chapter 6. A "Lot" of Trouble

CHOICES

Abram:

My nephew Lot and I both had large flocks and herds. Since the land just couldn't support all of us, I gave Lot a choice. I didn't want to quarrel with him or have our men quarreling over grazing land or waterholes, so even though I was his elder and the head of our small clan, I gave him the choice of land. If he went one way, I would go the other. Sometimes I wish I hadn't given him a choice. Especially later, when I saw the results of his choice.

Lot looked around and saw that the whole plain of the Jordan toward Zoar was well watered, like the garden of the LORD, like the land of Egypt. (This was before the LORD destroyed Sodom and Gomorrah.) So Lot chose for himself the whole plain of the Jordan and set out toward the east. The two men parted company. Abram lived in the land of Canaan, while Lot lived among the cities of the plain and pitched his tents near Sodom.   *(Genesis 13:8-12)*

Abram:

That wasn't the last I saw of Lot. After all, he was my nephew and such blood-ties are very important to my people.

CAPTURED, RESCUED

Sometime later the "kings" of several good-sized towns joined to fight another set of "kings", four against five. The head man of each large town was considered a king; for example, the king of Sodom, the king of Gomorrah, etc. You can see that these were local rulers, not kings over large territories.

This confederacy of four kings seized all the goods of Sodom and Gomorrah as well as all their food. Lot, who had moved into Sodom by then, and was very wealthy, was considered a special prize. They captured him and carried off his family and possessions. However, one man escaped and reported to me.

The times in which we lived were dangerous, so I had my own well-trained army of 318 men, all born in my household.

We chased the kidnappers up past the Sea of Kinnereth [Galilee] and all the way north to Dan. When we caught up with them, we carried out a night attack. I had split my men into two groups for the attack. We routed the other army and chased them way up north of Damascus. My men and I rescued Lot and all his possessions and women-folk and brought them back.

You would think Lot would realize that Sodom was not a good place to live, but he went right back there. Well, he was a grown man and he had to live with his own decisions, good or bad.

***

MELCHIZEDEK, KING OF SALEM

But something unusual, even odd, happened when we were coming back from the north. Melchizedek, who the king of Salem and also a priest of God Most High, came out to meet me, bringing bread and wine. He blessed me, saying:

Blessed be Abram by God Most High, ... who delivered your enemies into your hand. (Genesis 14:18-20)

I don't recall meeting him before this, or after, but I recognized that this priest worshiped the same God I did, although we used slightly different names for the Creator of heaven and earth. So I tithed to him a tenth of all the spoils of war we had gained.

Right after that I met the king of Sodom. He suggested I keep the spoils from the war, but give him the captured people. From what I had learned about his people, I wanted nothing to do with them or their goods, nor did I need wealth from him. And for sure I wasn't going to hand over my nephew and his household to him!

I guessed that Melchizedek's term, God Most High, would also be known to this man. I told him of my vow to the LORD, God Most High, Creator of heaven and earth, that I would accept nothing of his, not so much as the thong of a sandal, so he could never say he made me rich! No doubt it made him angry, but since he and his people owed their freedom to me and my fighting men, I wasn't worried.

Besides, I didn't have to live in his vicinity, as Lot did. God would take care of me. I had his promise that all the land I walked on would be given to me and my seed. *(Genesis 13:17)*

Chapter 7. Covenant with Abram

MY VERY GREAT REWARD

Not long after that, the word of the LORD came to me in a vision, saying, "Do not be afraid, Abram. I am your shield, your very great reward."

Shield, yes. I had seen many times how the LORD had shielded me—the situation in Egypt, for example—and I was thankful. But—reward? What greater reward could any man want than to have a son? Yet I was childless, and a servant in my household would be my heir.

The LORD took me outside and said, "Look up. Count the stars—if you can. Your offspring will be as numerous as the stars." And –I believed! My God does not lie. I believed and my God would supply.

But when He promised I would possess all this land, even though it was a lesser promise, I must admit I asked for proof.

He told me to prepare a ceremony with sacrifices, which I did. But then I fell into a deep sleep. God told me a fearful thing. It was worse than any nightmare. He said:

"Know for certain that for four hundred years your descendants will be strangers in a country not their own and that they will be enslaved and mistreated there.

But I will punish the nation they serve as slaves, and afterward they will come out with great possessions.

You, however, will go to your ancestors in peace and be buried at a good old age. In the fourth generation your descendants will come back here, for the sin of the Amorites has not yet reached its full measure."

On that day the LORD made a covenant with Abram and said, "To your descendants I give this land, from the Wadi of Egypt to the great river, the Euphrates...." Genesis 15:13-16, 18)

It is a hard thing to be told that your descendants would be enslaved for 400 years. But at least I would have descendants.

Eventually.   *(Abram)*

* * *

DOING IT MY WAY

Now Sarai, Abram's wife, had borne him no children. But she had an Egyptian slave named Hagar; so she said to Abram, "The LORD has kept me from having children. Go, sleep with my slave; perhaps I can build a family through her." (Genesis 16:1,2)

* * *

LIFE WITH SARAI

Hagar:

Mine was a common story in Egypt: too many mouths to feed, so sell the girl and let someone else feed her. When that foreigner bought me as a slave for his wife, I thought the gods had finally smiled on me. She was so beautiful, she looked just like a princess—which is what her name meant. I had no idea what life with Sarai would be like.

A slave has no rights. When my mistress says "Go," I must go, or be beaten.

I had heard them talking in the tent the night before. As usual, she was complaining. What did she have to complain about? Lots of servants to carry out her every whim. The wife of one of the richest men in the area. And he was so kind to her, even when she complained and fussed.

She was still good-looking even if she was getting old. But I often saw her frowning at her mirror. Her face was showing a few lines, and there was a hint of sag under the chin. Well, what did she expect at seventy-five? To look like a fifteen-year-old? Like me?

I had noticed her sizing me up. It made me uneasy. She was not cruel, but as far as I was concerned, neither was she a kind woman. Maybe beautiful rich women never have to learn how to be nice to people. Their beauty and wealth get them whatever they want. Well, almost anything. It hadn't gotten her a child and that was eating at her.

Anyway, I overheard them talking. She told Abram I could bear him a child in her place. It's done fairly often. Of course *I* would have no say about it. But he is even older than she is. And as his concubine, I could never hope to marry someone of my own age. What would *I* gain from this? Even my child would be considered hers, according to custom.

But of course I wasn't consulted. The next morning she said I was to go to his tent that night, and keep going until I became pregnant. I had no choice. I went because I had to.

I soon became pregnant. Everybody was thrilled. I was nauseated.

One day I was feeling especially sick and tired. When she told me to fetch her something, I snapped, "Get it yourself, old woman. I am bearing my lord's heir. You should be waiting on me."

I should have bit my tongue. For one her age, she has a strong arm, and I got it across the face. Then she stormed off to find Abram. The whole camp could hear her, "It's all your fault. I put my slave into your arms, and now that she's pregnant, she despises me."

Abram, as usual, tried to pacify her. "She's your servant," he said. "Do what you think is best."

After that, life really got unbearable. She found ways to make me work longer and harder, and rained blows on me if I hesitated. Finally I couldn't stand it anymore. Death in the desert was better than life with Sarai.

I ran away, with no more plan in my misery than to go back home to Egypt. I took the road to Shur, but the desert, I found, was more cruel than my mistress. I barely made it to the spring beside the road before collapsing. When I looked up from gulping water, I saw someone. I swear he hadn't been there a second earlier. He just appeared out of thin air. He was big and sort of blurry around the edges, or maybe it was because I was looking into the midday sun.

"Hagar, slave of Sarai" he said. Only, in our language, it came out "Runaway, slave of Princess." (Hagar means Flight or Runaway—which of course I was.) "Where have you come from, and where are you going?" he asked. I knew what was coming as soon as I said, "I've run away from my mistress." Sure enough, he said to go back and submit to Sarai. You don't argue with an angel, but in my mind I was crying, "She hates me. Surely she will kill me, one way or another."

He must have read my thoughts, or the fear in my face, for he gave me a promise. "You will have a son. You shall name him Ishmael [God hears], for the LORD has heard of your misery."

Abram had told me one night that the LORD had promised him descendants as many as the stars. Now the angel promised me that *my* descendants would be too many to count. Ah-ha, Sarai, what do you think of that!

I went back, but after that, every time Sarai scolded, I thought to myself, "My descendants will be too numerous to count. How about yours, old woman?" But I had learned the value of holding my tongue.

When the time came, I bore my master a son and Abram named him Ishmael, "God hears." I suppose Abram meant by the name that his God had heard his desire for a son, but the angel had told me to name my boy Ishmael because God heard of my affliction.

As I nursed my son, I was thankful that God had heard and seen my plight and rescued me. Ishmael was a fine boy, but the angel had warned that he would be as uncontrollable as a wild donkey. And he was—always in trouble, his hand against everyone. Well, yes, he was spoiled. Abram doted on him. After all, he was his only child, and the son of his old age.

All went fairly well for the next twelve or thirteen years.

(Hagar)

* * *

COVENANT SIGN, CIRCUMCISION

Abram:

Years passed. Now I had a son, Ishmael. Even though it was Sarai's idea to take Hagar to my bed, the situation caused ongoing strife. I confess, I did not handle that well.

Young Ishmael was spoiled, and it was my fault.

We moved around from place to place. You need water when you have large flocks and herds, and you have to keep looking for new pastures, so I had my men dig wells wherever we stopped for a length of time.

I continued to worship and wait for God's next appearance. When I was ninety-nine, he appeared to me again. "I am God Almighty; walk before me and be blameless," he said. Not an easy thing to do.

Always at the back of my mind were God's promises to me about descendants beyond counting and possession of vast lands. This was the first time the LORD referred to himself as El Shaddai, meaning God the Nourisher, the Strength-giver, the All-sufficient One. I wondered if maybe this name signified that his promises of descendants and vast possessions of lands was about to come true.

But no, not yet. This time, he expanded the promise that I would be the father of many nations and made a covenant with me.

First, he changed my name from Abram (exalted father) to Abraham (father of many), since I would be the father of many nations, he said, and even kings will be in my line. He would be God of "me and mine" for generations, and Canaan would be an everlasting possession.

After all these promises, he laid out my part: Every male must be circumcised, whether born into my household or bought; and newborns when they are eight days old. A covenant in the flesh.

God told me:

"My covenant in your flesh is to be an everlasting covenant. Any uncircumcised male, who has not been circumcised in the flesh, will be cut off from his people; he has broken my covenant." (Genesis 17:13,14)

Then he changed my wife's name from Sarai to Sarah. Both forms mean princess, but the name change indicates that she will be the mother of nations and even kings, even as the LORD had promised in our agreement. *(Abraham)*

Chapter 8. You're Kidding, Right?

ABRAHAM LAUGHS

Sarah? Barren Sarah the mother of nations? This struck me funny. I shouldn't have, but I fell down laughing. After all I was nearly 100 and Sarah 90! Whoever would imagine such a thing happening?

But even as I laughed at the very thought, God assured me that Sarah would indeed have a son. And God himself gave him his name: Isaac. Isaac, 'he laughs.' Don't tell *me* God doesn't have a sense of humor!

But I was also concerned about my son Ishmael. So when I said I hoped that Ishmael might also live under God's blessing, I was told that Ishmael would be blessed, be fruitful, have many descendants, be father of twelve rulers, and God will make him into a great nation, as well. But, God emphasized, this covenant we were making now was not concerned with Ishmael but with Isaac, whom Sarah will give birth to next year.

Did I hear him right? I'm no longer laughing. Just – dumbfounded. I shook my head in amazement, hardly noticing that God had gone from me.

Well, okay. In the meantime, there was something important I had to deal with immediately, the rite of circumcision. That very day my son Ishmael, every male whether born into my household or bought as slave, was circumcised. Myself, included.

Some time later we had unexpected visitors. I looked up and was surprised to see three men standing nearby. Hospitality requires that I invite them for a meal, and they accepted.

I hurried into the tent and told Sarah to make bread while I went and got a calf ready to eat. I also brought curds and milk for them, and stood by while they ate.

Then they asked me, "Where is your wife Sarah?"

"In the tent," I answered.

"I will surely return to you about this time next year," one of them said, "and Sarah your wife will have a son then." *(Abraham)*

* * *

SARAH LAUGHS

Now Sarah was listening at the entrance to the tent, which was behind him. ... Sarah laughed to herself as she thought, "After I am worn out and my master is old, will I now have this pleasure?"

Then the LORD said to Abraham, "Why did Sarah laugh and say, 'Will I really have a child, now that I am old?' Is anything too hard for the LORD? I will return to you at the appointed time next year and Sarah will have a son."   (Genesis 18:10,12-14)

* * *

THE DEVOTION OF LAUGHTER
by Betty Spence

Sarah was afraid, so she lied and said, "I did not laugh."
But He said, "Yes, you did laugh."   (Genesis 18:14)

You did too laugh, Sarah,
Wife of Abraham, friend of God,
barren, bearing Isaac, precious seed.
Who else, feeling for the first time
the baby move, could reverberate
such devotion as breaks yet
in ceaseless waves:
"Ah, ha-ha, Jehovah! Ah, ha-ha!"
            And your daughters: Hannah,
            Elizabeth, Mary ...
            like rays of hope breaking through
            faith's absurdities,

your joy catches, too, in their throats:
"Ah, ha-ha, Jehovah! A Son! A son!
You did too laugh, Sarah—
God heard your laughter rise
from disbelief to joyous praise.

He settles the barren woman in her home as a happy mother of children. Praise the LORD. (Psalm 113:9)

* * *

Abraham:

Sarah laughed at the idea, just as I had laughed, earlier. Having a child at our age would be a joke—if God ever jokes. Yet how appropriate was the name Isaac!

But our laughter (and disbelief) soon turned to horror. That meeting was not only to announce a miracle child. They had come to let me know what was about to happen to the wicked cities of Sodom and Gomorrah.

Chapter 9. Tale of Two Cities

BARGAINING WITH GOD

Then the LORD said, "The outcry against Sodom and Gomorrah is so great and their sin so grievous that I will go down and see if what they have done is as bad as the outcry that has reached me. If not, I will know. (Genesis 18:20)

Abraham:

I knew what the likely outcome would be. The sinful practices of those cities were well known to all of us in the area. But my nephew lived there. Would he be swept away, as well?

Hoping to avoid the slaughter of so many, yet in great fear, I dared to bargain with the LORD: If there were only fifty righteous in the city, would He spare it?

Yes, He would spare it for fifty.

How about if only 45 were righteous? Yes.

Forty? Thirty? Twenty? Yes. Yes. Yes.

Then I said, "Please don't be angry, but let me speak just once more. Surely You would spare the city if there were even ten."

After all, Lot lived there. There had to be at least ten in his household.

And the LORD said, "For the sake of ten, I will not destroy it."

(*Abraham*)

* * *

The two angels arrived at Sodom in the evening, and Lot was sitting in the gateway of the city. When he saw them, he got up to meet them. . . "My lords," he said, "please turn aside to your servant's house. You can wash your feet and spend the night and then go on your way early in the morning."

"No," they answered, "we will spend the night in the square." But he insisted. . . . Before they had gone to bed, all the men from every part of the city of

Sodom—both young and old—surrounded the house. They called to Lot, "Where are the men who came to you tonight? Bring them out to us so that we can have sex with them."

Lot went outside to meet them and shut the door behind him and said, "No, my friends. Don't do this wicked thing. Look, I have two daughters who have never slept with a man. Let me bring them out to you, and you can do what you like with them. But don't do anything to these men, for they have come under the protection of my roof."

"Get out of our way," they replied. "This fellow came here as a foreigner, and now he wants to play the judge! We'll treat you worse than them." They kept bringing pressure on Lot and moved forward to break down the door.

Lot's horrendous offer of his own daughters to the mob gives an in-depth look into the immorality running rampant in the city of Sodom.

What makes it even worse is that Lot knew better. He had spent many years with his uncle Abraham, and knew about the LORD and the righteous behavior God demands. So it horrifies us that Lot would consider his responsibility of safety for a guest more important than his responsibility for his own daughters' protection.

But this twisted offer helps us understand later when the girls themselves planned and carried out a plan to get their father drunk and became pregnant by him.

But the men inside reached out and pulled Lot back into the house and shut the door. Then they struck the men who were at the door of the house, young and old, with blindness so that they could not find the door.

The two men said to Lot, "Do you have anyone else here—sons-in-law, sons or daughters, or anyone else in the city who belongs to you? Get them out of here, because we are going to destroy this place. The outcry to the LORD against its people is so great that he has sent us to destroy it. (Genesis 19:1-13)

* * *

DAUGHTER OF SODOM

Daughter of Sodom was I, long before
I was wife to Lot, mother of daughters,
and "stepchild" (I guess you'd say)
to Jehovah, my husband's God.
      This stranger who had come to pitch
      his tent outside our town would be

a good match, my father said.
I could stand his eccentricities
since wealth went with them.
So, for fifteen years,
I've gone along with Lot,
his straitlaced moral code
and foreign worship rites,
so different from the codes and rites
we of Sodom have long observed.
My husband Lot's been good to me.
But always I seem caught between
my husband's and my people's ways.
He's respected for his wealth and yet
resented, for he lectures, scolds,
harangues the people in the streets:
"Thou shalt do this, shalt not do that!"
He's so set in these strange ways.
Why not relax his rigid code,
enjoy himself, and worry less what others do?
"You cannot force your ways on them,"
I say. "Your life to them seems bland,
unsavoury as salt-less bread."
Oh, that reminds me. We have guests.
My husband brought these two men home.
He'd met them at the city gate.
Though dinner's not quite done,
my two girls will help me serve—
they're learning how to be good wives.
Ah well, perhaps our guests will bring
excitement to our dull, staid lives.

* * *

So Lot went out and spoke to his sons-in-law, who were pledged to marry his daughters. He said, "Hurry and get out of this place, because the LORD is about to destroy the city!" But his sons-in-law thought he was joking.

With the coming of dawn, the angels urged Lot, saying, "Hurry! Take your wife and your two daughters who are here, or you will be swept away when the city is punished. ... Flee for your lives! Don't look back, and don't stop anywhere in the plain!" ... But Lot's wife looked back, and she became a pillar of salt.

Early the next morning Abraham got up and returned to the place where he had stood before the LORD. He looked down toward Sodom and Gomorrah,

toward all the land of the plain, and he saw dense smoke rising from the land, like smoke from a furnace.
So when God destroyed the cities of the plain, he remembered Abraham, and he brought Lot out of the catastrophe that overthrew the cities where Lot had lived. (Genesis 19:14-17,26-29)

Abraham:

My nephew and his daughters settled in the mountains. I would have given them shelter, but perhaps they were too ashamed, since both daughters were now pregnant by their father. The girls had been born and brought up in a place of "grievous sin" –that's how God put it. I suppose that explains their immoral plan to get their father drunk and then lay with him.

And maybe that explains why, after Lot lived for years in that city, there were not even ten righteous people there. When that hurts my heart, how much does it grieve a righteous God!

But as the saying goes, no man is wise at all hours, and that certainly includes me.

Chapter 10. Abraham, Sarah, and Isaac

"SHE'S MY SISTER" -- NOT AGAIN!

Abraham:

I moved over in the region of the Negev and stayed in Gerar, a city of the Philistines, for a while. And I did the same foolish thing I had done in Egypt. Hoping to save my own skin, I told them she was my sister. (I can't believe that I would do that—again!)

Sarah was indeed a beautiful woman—still is. You would never guess her age. And once again, she was taken into the king's household.

But God came to Abimelech in a dream one night and said to him, "You are as good as dead because of the woman you have taken; she is married." Now Abimelech had not gone near her, so he said, "Lord, will you destroy an innocent nation? Did he not say to me, 'She is my sister,' and didn't she also say, 'He is my brother?' I have done this with a clear conscience and clean hands."

Then God said to him in the dream, "Yes, I know. … Now return the man's wife, for he is a prophet, and he will pray for you and you will live."

(Genesis 20:3-7)

Well, the next morning I was summoned before Abimelech and it was the same as before in Egypt. I confessed that it was my fault completely. I had not trusted God to protect us; I had lied, told Sarah to lie also, and my sin caused trouble to many innocent people.

Before we left, I prayed for Abimelech and his wife and slaves so they could have children again; the LORD had kept all the women in Abimelech's household from conceiving because of Sarah.

I should not have gained financially for what I did, but Abimelech gave me sheep, cattle, and slaves of both sexes, plus a thousand shekels of silver. What do you do? You don't throw gifts back in a king's face.

I am thankful that I have a forgiving God. Still, I recognize that I have to live with the realization that I need an awful lot of forgiving.

But God is gracious to me and to Sarah, and He did for her what He had promised. The unimaginable came to pass. She was pregnant!

(*Abraham*)

* * *

HAGAR AND ISHMAEL TURNED OUT

Hagar:

The unthinkable happened. Sarai, at eighty-nine, became pregnant. If she was difficult before, she was now impossible! Ishmael was nothing, her son was everything!

One day after Isaac was weaned, she saw my Ishmael teasing her precious little boy. She demanded that Abram send us away. She actually said she didn't want Ishmael to inherit anything! It should all go to *her* son! Abram gave into her and set me and my son out on the road with no more than some bread and water. They threw us out like a worn-out sandal. There was no going back this time, I knew.

When our water was gone, Ishmael collapsed and crawled under a bush. I went off a little way because I couldn't bear to see him die. Then God's angel called from heaven again and said, "Hagar, don't be afraid. God has heard the boy crying. Help him up and take him by the hand, for I will make him into a great nation." Then my eyes were opened and I saw a well of water.

We went on and found a place to live in the Paran Desert. Ishmael grew up and became an expert with bow and arrow. I chose an Egyptian wife for him from among my own people. But as the angel had predicted, he is always fighting and being attacked by others.

I know, I know—God heard us. And I know that Abram's God rescued me from death –twice. My son's very name reminds me that God hears. But after the way Sarai and Abram treated me— discarding my son and me once they got what they really wanted all along—well, if that's how the worshipers of Jehovah act, you understand that I have trouble worshiping their God.

Life isn't easy for us now. But hard as it is—it's better than life
with Sarai.   *(Hagar)*

* * *

Abraham:

This land where God brought me and has promised to give me
forever is beautiful and —dry! Everywhere we went, lack of water was
a problem. I had my men dig wells in many places. Even when I was
in the coastal land of the Philistines, we dug wells.

The next time I had any dealings with Abimelech, he and Phicol
who commanded his forces, came to me with a proposition.
Apparently they hold me in a certain amount of fear, so they wanted
to make a treaty of fair dealings and mutual kindness. That sounded
fine to me, and I swore that I would show him the same kindness he
had shown me.

While we were there, I mentioned a situation where Abimelech's
servants had seized a well I had dug. He didn't know anything about
it, but was willing to deal with it. I gave him seven ewe lambs and
asked that he accept these as a witness that the well was one I had
dug.

We called that place Beersheba [Well of the Oath] because of the
oath we swore. And there I also called on the name of the LORD,
the Eternal God.

I stayed at Beersheba for a long time. My son Isaac was growing up
there. He was about seventeen when God came to me with a
command that froze my heart.

ABRAHAM'S TEST of FAITH

*"Take your son, your only son, whom you love—Isaac—and go to the region of
Moriah. Sacrifice him there as a burnt offering on a mountain I will show you."*
(Genesis 22:2)

How could God ask me to do this awful thing? This was the kind of
horror that other gods demanded. Not my God. Never *my* God.

I dared not tell Sarah. I dared not tell Isaac.

All I could do was follow God's orders. It was the hardest thing I
ever had to do in my life.

A doubt crept in—maybe the LORD really didn't love me. Maybe
he was my enemy, not my friend.

No. No, he had proved over and over that I and my son Isaac were precious to him. He assured me that he had great plans for my son's life.

My son's life. His …. Yes! His *life!* And the weak but growing hope filled my heart that this will not end in tragedy. God will do something—I don't know what—but something.

Oh Lord God. Help me. Help me.

I got up early—it's useless to put off doing what you must do— and saddled a donkey. I took Isaac and two servants with me. And wood. And a knife. And coals of fire, in a pot.

BECAUSE I MUST

It cannot be!
My son a sacrifice?
God detests such,
and yet He told me, "Offer up
your son, your only hope and promise."
It does no good to put it off.
God said I must.

I prepare to go,
cutting the wood to burn
the sacrifice, to burn my son.
Oh, God! my heart cries, No!
Yet I must, for God said so.

Three days' travel. Isaac's chatter
and excitement at the journey
rend my heart. He does not know.
He thinks this trip is fun.
For me each step is pain.
My heart cries, "Trust?"
It cannot be. Yet I must.

Servants left behind, we climb.
Isaac bears the wood
that soon will sear his flesh.
I bear the knife and pot of coals.
My mind flinches at the thought
that my own hand must wield

that knife, ignite the wood.
It's agony to obey.
Yet I must.
His question—where's the lamb?—
strikes like a sword.
The words spring to my lips
(not from my brain, I'm sure)
that one will be provided, yes,
God will provide himself . . . .
Whence came that thought?
But hope begins to burn away the dread.
If God had promised Isaac's birth, surely—

I can't conceive of good from this!
What will his mother say?
But maybe . . . maybe God . . .
I can but trust, for I must
or die from pain, myself.

God does not spare me, even to
the binding of my son, raising the knife
to cut his throat (as with a lamb).
I cannot look into his eyes.
My own are blind with tears.
The muscles in my upraised arm
quiver, fight against the deed.
But as the knife begins its downward thrust
a voice—a blessed voice—calls, "Stop!"

God is satisfied, he says,
that, dearly as I love my son,
I love and honor Yahweh more.
The sacrifice—a ram caught in the thorns—
was provided, as I said.
Henceforth, no matter what,
I will trust
simply because I must.

So Abraham called that place The LORD Will Provide. (Genesis 22:14)

Chapter 11. Isaac's Mother, Isaac's Bride

A GRAVE FOR SARAH

Sarah lived to be a hundred and twenty-seven years old. She died at Kiriath Arba (that is, Hebron) in the land of Canaan, and Abraham went to mourn for Sarah and to weep over her.

Then Abraham rose from beside his dead wife and spoke to the Hittites. He said, "I am a foreigner and stranger among you. Sell me some property for a burial site here so I can bury my dead." *(Genesis 23:1-4)*

Abraham:

When a man is in the midst of mourning, it is not a good time to haggle over money. But that almost happened when I tried to buy a place to bury Sarah.

First, the Hittites complimented me, saying I was a great leader, and I could have the best place to bury my wife. I had picked out a cave at the edge of a field. I bowed respectfully and asked the elders if they would speak to Ephron, the owner, for me and ask him to sell me his cave. I intended to pay the full price.

Ephron was sitting there and he said, "No, no. I will give you the land and the cave that is in it, with these people as witnesses. Bury your dead wife."

That sounded good, but I hesitated. Maybe I'm overly suspicious, but I could imagine that someday they might decide that since I hadn't officially bought it, it really wasn't mine. And then I would not be able to visit Sarah's grave or have the right to be buried beside her.

I answered Ephron, "Please let me pay you the full price for the field. Accept my money, and I will bury my dead there."

48

The price he quoted seemed out of reason for just a cave: ten pounds of silver! But, as I said, it is not a good time to haggle. Besides, my Sarah was worth much more than mere silver, so I agreed. They counted it out by weight, just as traders normally do, and the elders were witnesses that I had bought Ephron's field, the cave, and all the trees in the field.

So I buried my beloved Sarah. I will join her soon, I hope. At least my descendants now have a place to lay our dead.   *(Abraham)*

* * *

Abraham was now very old, and the LORD had blessed him in every way. He said to the senior servant in his household, "Put your hand under my thigh.* I want you to swear by the LORD, the God of heaven and earth, that you will not get a wife for my son from the daughters of the Canaanites, among whom I am living, but will go to my country and my own relatives and get a wife for my son Isaac."   (Genesis 24:1-4)

*a custom showing you will keep the promise

* * *

A BRIDE FOR ISAAC

Eliezer:

It was a sign of his regard for me that my master sent me to pick out a bride for his son Isaac. I've been with Abram, or Abraham as they are calling him now, for many years—long before Isaac was born. At one time because my master was childless, the plan was that I would be his heir. But then the unimaginable happened. His wife Sarah, although ninety years old, actually bore him a child!

And what a blessing that child has been. We all love Isaac. He is a gentle soul. In many ways he's a lot like his father, a God-fearing man. But since his mother Sarah died, he seems—oh, I don't know—a bit lost or sad. Anyway, Abraham decided he needed a wife. After all, Isaac is forty; it's time he married and gave Abraham some grandchildren. My master is a hundred and forty, and you know how important grandchildren are to us older people.

Isaac hasn't shown any interest in the local girls, and to tell the truth, Abraham would never let him marry any of these idol-worshipping Canaanite women, anyway. My master wants someone from among his own relatives back in Aram Naharim.

My master bound me with an oath that I am to pick a wife for Isaac. "What should I do?" I ask him. "If the girl doesn't want to come back with me, should I then take Isaac to her home country?"

"No! By no means should you take my son back there!" he said. "If the girl won't come back with you, then you will be free from this promise. But you must not take my son back there."

So imagine the situation with me: here I am with my men and ten camels laden down with all kinds of beautiful things my master is sending to his relatives. We've finally arrived in Northwest Mesopotamia and at the town where Abraham's brother Nahor lives. It's late in the day, we're tired, hungry, thirsty—especially thirsty. So we stop at the village well.

During this whole trip I've been turning this over in my mind: how on earth can I know which girl is the right one? The only plan I could come up with is to ask God to show me which girl he has for Isaac. So here I am beside the well, and praying:

"LORD, God of my master Abraham, make me successful today, and show kindness to my master Abraham. See, I am standing beside this spring, and the daughters of the townspeople are coming out to draw water. May it be that when I say to a young woman, 'Please let down your jar that I may have a drink,' and she says, 'Drink, and I'll water your camels too'—let her be the one you have chosen for your servant Isaac. By this I will know that you have shown kindness to my master." (Genesis 24:12-14)

Just as I open my eyes after praying, I see this beautiful young woman coming up the steps from the spring with a full jar of water. "Would you be willing to lower your jar and give a thirsty traveler a drink?" I ask.

"Gladly," she says. And while I drink, she says, "If you are thirsty, your camels must be thirsty too. I will draw water from the well for them." And she begins to water my camels! And I can tell you, ten camels can drink a lot!

"I thank you for your kindness," I say, rejoicing at God's immediate answer to my prayer. I watch quietly while she waters them. When the camels finish drinking, I give her the gold ring and two heavy gold bracelets which Abraham had sent as bride-gifts.

When she accepts them, a bit puzzled, I ask, "Who is your father? Does he have room to put up my men and me for the night?"

She says, "My father is Bethuel, the son of Milcah and Nahor. And yes, we have straw for your camels and a place where you can stay."

I bow and worship the LORD, thanking Him for leading me to my master's relatives. Then I introduce myself, "I am Eliezer, chief servant of Abraham, son of Terah."

She interrupts, "Oh, you must mean Great-uncle Abram! My grandfather Nahor has often spoken of his brother. Oh, I must go and tell my family!" And she runs off, leaving us still at the well. *What a sweetheart she is! I think. I believe she would be a good match for Isaac.*

A few minutes later a man comes running toward me. It is her brother Laban. He had seen the ring and the bracelets on his sister's arms, and heard her story of the man at the spring. He politely invites me, "Come, you who are blessed by the LORD. Why stand here? I have prepared a place for you and for your camels, and a meal is ready for us to eat together."

After making arrangements for the men with me, I accept Laban's invitation to supper. But until I tell them the whole story, I can't accept their hospitality or eat their food. I describe my master's wealth, explain his desire to find a wife for Isaac among his relatives; and, most amazing of all to me, I tell them how quickly and precisely God had answered my prayer.

I am astonished when her brother Laban and her father Bethuel immediately say, "This is clearly from the LORD. . . . Rebekah is yours. Take her and go. Let her marry your master's son, as the LORD has commanded." It must be the LORD God moving in their hearts to let them send their beautiful Rebekah away with me.

Having accomplished my task for Abraham, I want to head home the next morning, but her family asks me to delay at least ten days. Certainly it's understandable; they would like some time to get used to the idea of their daughter going far away, to a home of her own, where it was likely that they would never get to see her again. But they leave it up to Rebekah whether to go immediately or wait ten days. She is eager to go and meet her husband-to-be, so they send her with me, with their blessing.

In my many years in the tents of Abraham, I had seen several miraculous things happen. Sarah's pregnancy at age 90, for instance. But this time I am personally in the midst of one, as I see God moving in remarkable ways, to bring about His purposes. I feel as if my head is spinning.

The very next morning Rebekah, her servant girls, and I mount up and head south to where my master and his son are waiting. Understandably, Rebekah has many questions about her future bridegroom, and I use the travel time to "introduce" Isaac to his bride.

I think they will be a good match—especially since it is so evident that the LORD GOD brought this about.   *(Eliezar)*

Then Rebekah and her attendants got ready and mounted the camels and went back with the man. So the servant took Rebekah and left. Now Isaac had come from Beer Lahai Roi, for he was living in the Negev. He went out to the field one evening to meditate, and as he looked up, he saw camels approaching. Rebekah also looked up and saw Isaac. She got down from her camel and asked the servant, "Who is that man in the field coming to meet us?"

"He is my master," the servant answered. So she took her veil and covered herself. Then the servant told Isaac all he had done. Isaac brought her into the tent of his mother Sarah, and he married Rebekah. So she became his wife; and he loved her; and Isaac was comforted after his mother's death.

(Genesis 24:61-67)

Chapter 12. Isaac and the Wells

THE DEATH OF ABRAHAM

Abraham had taken another wife, whose name was Keturah. She bore him [six sons]. … Abraham left everything he owned to Isaac, But while he was still living he gave gifts to the sons of his concubines and sent them away from his son Isaac to the land of the east.

Abraham lived a hundred and seventy-five years. Then Abraham breathed his last and died at a good old age, an old man and full of years; and he was gathered to his people. His sons Isaac and Ishmael buried him in the cave of Machpelah near Mamre, in the field of Ephron son of Zohar the Hittite, the field Abraham had bought from the Hittites. There Abraham was buried with his wife Sarah.

After Abraham's death, God blessed his son Isaac, who then lived near Beer Lahai Roi.   *(Genesis 25:1,2,5-11)*

* * *

Rebekah:

When Isaac and I were married, my father-in-law was a hundred and forty. He was as anxious for a child from our union as we ourselves were. Perhaps more anxious, considering that it had taken Sarah and him more than twenty-five years to have Isaac. But he was not to live long enough to see Isaac's child—or children, as it turned out.

Ours was truly a love match, but there was no child to bless our union (not from lack of trying). Isaac told me that his own mother had been considered barren, but finally had him when she was ninety. I couldn't help wondering (or dreading) if that would be my fate. But I must admit I also wondered if perhaps it was *my* fault. That is a hard thing to bear.

I remembered my family's blessing on me when I left my hometown of Nahor. They had said: *"Our sister, may you increase to thousands upon thousands; may your offspring possess the cities of their enemies."* The memory began to have a bitter taste. Thousands of offspring? We couldn't even have one.

It probably wasn't the fault of Isaac's line. His father had other children by his concubines. Maybe it was her fault, Sarah's fault, in that case.

But God had promised, and we clung to that promise. For twenty years, we clung to that promise!   *(Rebekah)*

* * *

ISAAC'S COVENANT WITH GOD

Isaac:

My father had told me about a famine time when he went down to Egypt, and claimed that my mother Sarah was his sister. Actually, he did that again in Gerar of the Philistines. He was ashamed that he had shown a lack of trust in the LORD in those two instances. You'd think I would know better!

But maybe it's like father, like son, because I did the very same thing. It was famine time, but the LORD had appeared to me and told me not to go down to Egypt, but to stay here. I went to Gerar, city of the Philistines in the coastal lands along the Mediterranean.

But while I was there, the LORD appeared to me and made a covenant with me. It mirrored the agreement that Father told me God had made with him. The LORD told me:

Do not go down to Egypt; live in the land where I tell you to live. Stay in this land for a while, and I will be with you and will bless you. For to you and your descendants I will give all these lands and will confirm the oath I swore to your father Abraham. I will make your descendants as numerous as the stars in the sky and will give them all these lands, and through your offspring all nations on earth will be blessed, because Abraham obeyed me and did everything I required of him, keeping my commands, my decrees, and my instructions.
(Genesis 26:2-5)

"SHE'S MY SISTER"

So, because of the famine we went to Gerar. The king was Abimelech—oddly enough, that's the same name as the king my father had dwelt with years before. I'm not sure, but this Abimelech was either the son or grandson of the previous one.

My wife Rebekah is very beautiful, and men noticed her. But I did the same stupid thing my father had done; I said she was my sister because I feared they might kill me in order to get my beautiful wife.

We had been living in Gerar a long time, but one day the king looked out a window and saw me caressing my wife. (Not a good thing for us to do, even in our own private garden where someone could see.) He summoned me and accused me: "She's really your wife! Why did you tell me she's your sister?" I had to confess that I was afraid of being killed.

Well, he was angry. Someone might have slept with her and brought guilt on his people, he said. Those Philistines had a better moral code than I had given them credit for, and I was ashamed. The king gave strict orders not to harm me or my wife, on pain of death. It looked like all was well, for a while.

I planted crops that year and had a bumper crop. My wealth grew, both in crops and flocks and herds and servants. I became the object of envy. I also became a target. My father's servants had dug several wells while he lived in Gerar. Mysteriously the wells were stopped up, filled with dirt. And then Abimelech told me I was no longer welcome in his city. I had become too powerful for them, he said.

When the king tells you to leave, you leave.

* * *

DIGGING WELLS, MAKING TREATIES

We left the city of Gerar and settled farther away, in the Valley of Gerar. I set my servants to reopening the wells that had been dug in my father's time. The Philistines had stopped up those in the valley too. When the wells were cleared I gave them the same names my father had used.

Water is vital, so where my servants dug in that valley, they discovered a well of fresh water. That became a source of fighting between my herders and the herders of Gerar. "Our land, our water," they claimed–even though we had dug it. I named that well Esek, "dispute."

My men dug another well and it also was a source of quarrels so I named that one Sitnah, "enmity."

I moved on and we dug yet another well. Nobody quarreled over that one—wonderful! So I named it Rehoboth, meaning "room enough" saying, "Now the LORD has made room for us, and we will be successful in this land." We then moved on to Beersheba.

That night the LORD appeared to him and said, "I am the God of your father Abraham. Do not be afraid, for I am with you; I will bless you and will increase the number of your descendants for the sake of my servant Abraham."

Isaac built an altar there and called on the name of the LORD. There he pitched his tent, and there his servants dug a well. (Genesis 26:23-25)

We had made a camp at a place we came to call Beersheba. While my men were working on yet another well, I had visitors. Abimelech came with Ahuzzah his personal advisor and Phicol, the commander of his army. I bluntly asked, "Why have you come to me, since you were hostile to me and sent me away?"

It seems they had been considering the evident blessing of the LORD on me, and decided it would be wise to make a treaty, a non-aggression pact, with someone whom the LORD had clearly blessed. They also reminded me that they had always treated me well and had sent me away in peace. (That's one way of putting it, I guess.)

Anyway, I agreed, and made a feast for them. Early the next morning we swore an oath of mutual respect before they went peacefully on their way.

Two oaths in one day! One with the LORD and one with Abimelech and his people. And then, yet another blessing! That very day my servants came and told me, "We have found good water!" in the well they were digging.

A time for rejoicing! I called this well Shibah (meaning "oath,"), so the town is Beersheba, Well of the Oath.

My servants have become experts in digging wells. Some wells go down to the depth of 65 feet or more. It's dangerous work because cave-ins can happen. I wonder if I will be known in future generations as Isaac the Well-Digger. A good well is a blessing. *(Isaac)*

Chapter 13. Twins At War

ANSWERED PRAYER

Rebekah:

Twenty years of waiting and hoping. Twenty years, and still no child.

But then Isaac prayed to the LORD for me. He had prayed before, but maybe the time wasn't right. Anyway, God answered his prayer—and my prayer—finally! To our great joy, I found I was pregnant. But when I began to feel the child moving, it seemed more than the usual occasional kick that other mothers had described. I couldn't figure out why there seemed to be a war inside me. What was going on? Why was this happening to me?

So I went to ask the LORD about it, and he told me:

"Two nations are in your womb, and two peoples from within you will be separated; one people will be stronger than the other, and the older will serve the younger." (Genesis 25:23)

It *was* a war and I was the battleground! The LORD said I was carrying two children, twins. And he also was telling us about the future of my two boys, and even what would happen many years later.

The battle in my womb continued until the day they were born. You can imagine that I was very, very glad when they finally were born.

Some twins look alike. Mine were very different. The first to be born was red and hairy all over, so he was named Esau which means 'hairy.' He was often called Edom, as well, which means 'red.'

When the next child came out, his hand was gripping Esau's heel, so he was named Jacob, which sounds like 'heel.' To grab the heel means to trick or supplant. I fear that his name influenced his character.

(I don't think we ever told the boys that the LORD had said "the older will serve the younger." That would really be asking for trouble. Yet, known or unknown, it played out in their lives.)

As the boys grew up, Esau loved the outdoors and was a skillful hunter. My husband was very fond of wild game, and partly for that reason, he loved Esau best. (I wonder at that, for Isaac's gentle disposition seemed the opposite of Esau's contentious spirit.).

I know, we shouldn't have favorites, but we both did, and Jacob was mine. Although he worked with the flocks and herds, he learned to make a delicious lentil stew. And that played a part in what Jacob did to his brother. It came about this way:

Esau came in from hunting, saying, "I'm about to die from hunger," and Jacob said, "I'll trade a bowl of stew for your birthright."

"What good is a birthright if you're dead of hunger?" Esau said. "Come on, Jacob, give me something to eat."

"I said, I'll give you some stew if you promise you'll give me the birthright."

"Yeah, yeah. You can have it. Now give me some stew."

Well, obviously he didn't value it as he should.

Nor did he value our advice to go north to get a wife from my own people up in Northeastern Mesopotamia. Instead, Esau married two Hittite women from the area. They brought much sorrow to us. I can't describe how greatly they provoked me, day after day! I told Isaac, "If Jacob also marries a Hittite woman, I want to die!" But so far Jacob didn't show any desire to marry. *(Rebekah)*

* * *

THE STOLEN BLESSING

Esau:

It seemed impossible for me to please my mother. I married two women, thinking they would be a help to her around the house—or tent. They couldn't please her either, maybe because they were mine. After a while, they stopped trying. Just as I stopped trying to please her.

Her favorite was Jacob, smooth-skinned, namby-pamby Jacob.

Father had all the problems that accompany aging. He was just about blind, and his hearing was failing too. But he still had a good appetite for the wild game I hunted.

One day he called me to his tent and told me:

I am now an old man and don't know the day of my death. Now then, get your equipment—your quiver and bow--and go out to the open country to hunt some wild game for me. Prepare me the kind of tasty food I like and bring it to me to eat, so that I may give you my blessing before I die."   *(Genesis 27:2-4)*

That birthright business with Jacob was years ago. I'd almost forgotten about it, no one had mentioned it again, and I didn't think anyone had told Father. Maybe everyone else had forgotten and I was about to get the birthright blessing, the double share. After all, I am the firstborn and it's my right to have it.

I gathered up my bow and arrows and went out to hunt.

(Esau)

* * *

Rebekah:

I was listening when Isaac told Esau to kill some wild game for him to eat, and afterward he would bless him. Had Isaac forgotten that the LORD had told me 'the older would serve the younger'? Indeed, Isaac was getting forgetful in his old age, so maybe he had forgotten—or decided to bless his favorite son anyway.

Well, I would put a stop to that! If God wasn't doing it the way he had promised me, I would help him out! And since Esau would be away hunting, I had time to figure out what I could do to set things right, the way they should be. The way God had promised.

I called Jacob and told him what I had heard. Then I said, "Go out and get two of our best young goats. I will prepare them just the way your father likes them. Then you take the food to your father, and he will bless *you* before he dies."

Jacob was ready to do it, but he said it wouldn't work if his father touched him. Isaac would expect to feel Esau's hairy skin, whereas Jacob's was smooth, and then, instead of blessing him, Isaac would curse him because of being tricked.

"Just do what I tell you," I said. "If your father curses you, I accept the blame. Now go get the goats."

I hastily prepared the meat, and while it was cooking, I found some of Esau's best clothes for Jacob to put on.

Hairy. Let's see. What can I do about that? My hand rested on the skins from the baby goats. Yes! They would feel like hairy Esau. I fitted them around Jacob's arms and neck, gave him the cooked meat and some fresh bread.

"There!" I said. "Now go in to your father. I'll keep watch for Esau. Go!" *(Rebekah)*

* * *

Jacob:

It worked. I fooled my father into thinking I was my brother. He seemed suspicious at first, asking how I found the meat so quickly, so I said the LORD God had helped me.

He reached out to touch me, then said, "Your voice sounds like Jacob's voice, but your hands are hairy like Esau's." I was glad my mother had thought to put the kid's skin on my arms, or he would certainly have guessed that I wasn't my brother.

He still seemed to need to check, saying, "Are you really my son Esau?" and I lied again, "Yes, I am."

He seemed to accept that, and ate the food and drank the wine I gave him.

But then he put me through one more test. "My son, come near and kiss me." And, thanks to my mother's plan for me to wear Esau's clothing, the smell of his clothing convinced Father and he blessed me, saying:

The smell of my son is like the smell of the field that the LORD has blessed. May God give you heaven's dew and earth's richness—an abundance of grain and new wine. May nations serve you and peoples bow down to you. Be lord over your brothers, and may the sons of your mother bow down to you. May those who curse you be cursed, and those who bless you be blessed." (Genesis 27:27-29)

I walked out, scarcely able to contain my joy. What an all-inclusive blessing! And he also had said my mother's sons will bow down to me! Yes!

Yes, it was a stolen blessing, and I had lied to get it. But it was worth whatever I had to do. After all, hadn't the LORD told my mother that "the elder shall serve the younger"? So if we had to help the LORD a little, what did it matter in the end?   *(Jacob)*

* * *

Esau:

I came in, skinned what I taken in hunting, and prepared it. While it cooked, I kept thinking about the blessing my father had for me.

When the meat was cooked, I took it in and said, "Father, rise and eat the food that your son killed for you and then bless me."

When Father asked, "Who are you?" I was confused. Although he was blind and nearly deaf, his mind seemed sharp as usual. What did he mean, who am I?

"I am your son—your firstborn son—Esau," I answered.

Father began to tremble. With head and hands shaking as a tree shakes in a storm, he said, "Then who was that who brought me food before you came? I ate it, and I blessed —I blessed *him*. Oh no. I blessed the wrong one. It's too late now. I can't take back my blessing."

I felt as if I had been struck in the heart by one of my own arrows. No! No! "Bless me—me, too, my father!" I cried.

"It was Jacob. Your brother came and tricked me. He has taken your blessing." Tears ran down his face, and he seemed to fold in on himself. For the first time he looked helpless, hopeless.

I tried to control the rage that boiled up within me. "Oh, how appropriate is that scoundrel's name! Jacob the Cheater, the Usurper! He has tricked me these two times. He has stolen my share of everything you own, and now ... Now he has taken my blessing!" I turned to my father, imploring, "Haven't you saved any blessing for me?" and I almost said, but restrained myself, 'I'm your favorite son.'

Father said, "I gave Jacob the power to be master over you, and all his brothers will be his servants. And I kept him strong with grain and new wine. There is nothing left to give you, my son."

I pleaded, "Do you have only one blessing, Father?" and I began to cry aloud.

Father drew himself up, reached out his hand to me, and blessed me, saying,

"Your dwelling will be away from the earth's richness, away from the dew of heaven above. You will live by the sword, and ..." His voice shook as he said, *"and you will serve your brother. But... but when you grow restless, you will throw his yoke from off your neck." (Genesis 27:39,40)*

So that was my blessing! Servant to my brother, living in arid places, living by the sword. And a promise that one day I would break free. Some blessing!

Well, Father is old and will die soon. When he dies, I will properly mourn him. Then, when it will no longer bring pain to my father, I will kill my cheating brother.

It won't change what he did, but if he is dead without issue, how can all those fine blessings he stole from me come to pass? Who knows? They may come back onto me, and maybe that will count as "breaking free" of him.   *(Esau)*

* * *

Rebekah:

Esau made no secret that he planned to kill Jacob. They constantly circled each other like dogs ready to fight.

I might have known it would lead to this. And Isaac figured out that I had a part in the whole mess, and that built a wall between us.

Yet I couldn't regret that Jacob had the blessing, no matter how he got it. But I didn't want to see him dead, so I told him what Esau was planning. "You'll be safe with my brother Laban up in Haran. I'll get your father to send you up there. When Esau cools down, I'll send a servant to tell you it's safe to come home. I don't want to lose both sons on the same day."

But I had to make up a reason for Isaac to send Jacob to my family, so I said, "These Hittite women that Esau married are more than I can stand! I would rather die if Jacob wants to marry one of these Hittite women too. Can you do something? Maybe send him up to my brother Laban?"

So Isaac sent for Jacob and told him he must not marry a Canaanite woman. And he sent him to my brother Laban with a blessing:

May God Almighty bless you and make you fruitful and increase your numbers until you become a community of peoples. May he give you and your descendants the blessing given to Abraham, so that you may take possession of the land where you now reside as a foreigner, the land God gave to Abraham.
(Genesis 28:3,4)

I hated to see him go even though it was the best we could do. I often imagine the day that I'll see my beloved son and his wife and, maybe, children. I certainly hope my son will not have to wait as many years before having children like his father and grandfather did.

So I wait and hope. *(Rebekah)*

* * *

Esau:

I heard that my father had blessed Jacob—again!— and sent him off to Paddam Aram, to get a wife from Mother's family. He also had commanded him not to marry a Canaanite

Well, I finally realized that Father did not want us to marry local women. But I already had two Hittite wives, Oholibamah and Adah. I thought it would please Father so I went to Uncle Ishmael, and married his daughter Basemath. I don't know that she pleased my parents any better, but at least I tried.

It would be years before I saw Jacob again. In the meantime my family grew. While I was living in the mountains of Edom, I was blessed with flocks and lands. Oh, did I tell you that Edom was named after me? I've gone by both names for years: Esau means hairy and Edom means red, and I was both at my birth.

It will give you an idea of my wealth if I tell you that the next time Jacob and I were face to face, I had 400 men behind me. Now that's an interesting story, but I'll save that for later. *(Esau)*

Chapter 14. Jacob's Encounters

MY SIDE OF THE STORY

Jacob:

I worshiped the LORD God, of course, with the rest of the family, but I didn't think he approved of me, not like my father and grandfather who both had a special relationship with the LORD. In the family it is said that Abraham was God's friend. Seven times the LORD spoke to my grandfather Abraham, and even visited his tent once.

When I was a child, Grandfather told me many times about leaving Ur and coming to this land. "You must remember these stories and pass them along to your children," he told me. My own father, Isaac, was twice spoken to by Jehovah, confirming the covenant God had made with Grandfather.

But somehow, I never expected the LORD to speak to me. I wasn't godly like my father and grandfather. It was easy to blame my shortcomings on my position as second son or even on my name, Jacob. It means Usurper or Cheater, one who gains by force or trickery. I was named that because when I was born, I came forth grasping my twin brother Esau's heel.

Mother said we started fighting in the womb and never stopped. Esau called me "Mama's Boy" so I came back at him with "Daddy's Little Man." You would think that growing up where each parent had a favorite, I would know better, but later I did the same thing with my own sons, and that almost led to murder. Dysfunction breeds true.

Anyway, from hearing Jacob the Cheater or Jacob the Trickster a hundred times a day, I learned to fit my name. Don't you find that we're likely to become what we're called? Parents need to be careful what they name their kids –another lesson I should have learned and didn't, when I let my children be named by their mothers. The boys have some strange names: Reuben means behold, a son; Simeon – one who hears; Levi – joined; Judah – praise; Dan – he who judges; Naphtali – my struggle; Gad – good fortune; Asher – happy; Issachar – reward; Zebulun – dwelling; Joseph – may God add. I was responsible for Benjamin's name because I didn't name him exactly as Rachel wanted, but that is a story for later.

I was really good at was wrestling, and I won a local fame. The unexpected moves and strength inherent in my name were qualities I used to win—until that night I met my match.

But confession is good for the soul, so let me fill you in on the background. With my mother's connivance, I tricked my brother Esau out of his double-portion inheritance as oldest son, and my father's blessing. (You gotta know, Esau didn't think it was all that important until I stole it.) He was furious and threatened to kill me. To get me out of harm's way, my parents sent me up north to my mother's family.

Maybe they also hoped I'd do some serious thinking about my life and my methods of getting what I want. So far, "I want what I want when I want it" would describe me. I never put anyone else's needs or rights before those of mine. If I wanted it that was enough reason to do whatever it took to get it. Hard-headed, underhanded, selfish. And God? I really hadn't bothered to ask his approval on anything I did. It never occurred to me that he had anything special planned for me. I didn't listen to him and I figured he wasn't paying any attention to me. Oh boy! Was I wrong!

BETHEL DREAMS AND BARGAINS

It was on that journey that God showed me he had great plans for me and my descendants. (Me, the one with no plans and no descendants.) I had left Beersheba, but when night came, I slept out under the stars. I've done that hundreds of times, but this night I dreamed of a ladder stretching from earth up into heaven. A stairway for angels.

Then I saw the LORD standing at the top and he spoke to me:

I am the LORD, the God of your father Abraham and the God of Isaac. I will give you and your descendants the land on which you are lying. Your descendants will be as many as the dust of the earth. ... All the families of the earth will be blessed through you and your descendants.

I am with you and will protect you everywhere you go and will bring you back to this land. I will not leave you until I have done what I have promised you.   (Genesis 28:13-15)

When I woke up, I was scared! "Surely God is in this place and I didn't know it! This place frightens me. It must be the house of God, the gate of heaven." (After that, we called that place Bethel, 'house of God.')

I took the stone I had used for a pillow, set it up, and poured olive oil on it, as an altar. Then I made God a promise—well, I guess it actually was more of a bargain. I'm good at bargaining. Just ask Esau. Or maybe you shouldn't.

Anyway, I told God what *I* wanted: that h would be with me, protect me on this journey, provide food and clothes so I could return home. And if he does these things, I'll take him as my God. Oh yeah, and I'll give back a tenth of everything he gives me. That was my bargain.

Looking back on it, I can't believe that I did that. That's no way to treat the God of the universe. My father and grandfather would never do such a thing! But God kept his promise, while I kept my end of the bargain. Sort of.

JACOB THE FAMILY MAN

I was heading for my mother's people in Haran. In this field I saw a well and three flocks of sheep lying near it. While I was talking with the shepherds, this beautiful girl came up with her father's sheep. I had asked them if they knew Laban, and they said, "Here comes his daughter Rachel."

I was all for sliding the cover off to let her water her sheep so she could take them back to pasture.

"Oh no," the shepherds said. "We can't do that until all the sheep are here." Custom, it seemed, was stronger than need or common sense. It was only noon, and the sheep usually gathered to be watered at the end of the day. Well, I couldn't see making her and her thirsty sheep wait just because of "custom," so I rolled the stone off and watered her sheep.

Then I introduced myself as the son of her father's sister, Rebekah, and I kissed her (on the forehead, of course). And that is how I met my lovely Rachel.

I worked for her father for a month without pay (that way I could get to see Rachel), but then Laban said, "Just because you are a relative of mine, should you work for nothing? What would you like for your wages?" (Ha! He opened the door and I walked in.)

"Let me marry your younger daughter Rachel. If you will, I'll work seven years for you." Laban agreed, so I worked for him for seven years, and it seemed but a few days, because I loved her so much.

But Laban, tricky conniver that he is, decided to get his older daughter Leah off his hands first.   *(Jacob)*

* * *

DISCONTENT IN THE TENT

Leah:

When I first saw Jacob, I liked what I saw. But it was not to be—he had eyes for no one but my sister. And I understood. I'm not beautiful like she is. I've spent my whole life, since she was born, being the plain big sister, the one told to take care of cute little Rachel.

He saw her first—but that wouldn't have mattered anyway. And I knew that he and Rachel would marry, eventually. My father had told him if he worked for him seven years, he could marry his daughter. (I wonder if, way back then, Father had planned the switch. It would be just like him.)

The seven years were up and the whole house was full of excitement. The wedding tent was set up, ready for the bridal night. Food and wine were laid out in abundance, and Rachel was excited beyond words. She had shown all her friends the dress made especially for her wedding.

So in the midst of all the wedding excitement, I was told to go to my mother's room. As I reached the door, Rachel rushed out and nearly ran me down. My eyes are not strong, but I was sure she was weeping. When she saw me, she cried, "I hate you!"

Puzzled, I watched her run off into the room we shared. *Why does she hate me? I haven't done anything to her. Well, maybe it's just wedding nerves.* I shrugged, and went in my mother's room and learned why my sister hates me. My father is—well, underhanded, and although no one says it out loud, at least around us, it is well known. I was to be the bride tonight in my sister's place.

I felt sorry for Rachel, but I couldn't deny a bit of excitement. A blessing I had never imagined possible would be mine. But I also knew my relationship with my sister could never be the same. I didn't realize how deep the chasm between us would be. Our life from that moment would be a constant strife.

I wondered how the substitution could be carried out without Jacob knowing, but Father had worked it out. The bride was to be heavily veiled, and of course there was no light in the bridal tent.

There's a saying, "What's begun in deceit seldom ends with delight." I was called "Rachel darling" on my wedding night. You can't imagine the pain of that.

After he fell asleep, I wept, dreading daybreak when he would see who was in his bed. And he was, to put it mildly, furious! Who could blame him? But to me it was the ultimate rejection as he stormed off to confront my father.

Oh yes, Jacob had to finish out my bridal week. No joy –for him or for me. Father had made Jacob promise to work another seven years, so after my week was complete, my sister got her wedding after all. *(Leah)*

* * *

Jacob:
Laban thought it was unlikely anyone would ever marry Leah, plain and near-sighted as she is. She's not exactly ill-favored, but . . . Oh well, he switched brides, and I didn't realize it until the next morning. I could have killed him! But Laban smooth-talked me into marrying them both. The only hitch was that I had to work seven more years. I suppose some would say I was getting my own back— the trickster being tricked—but that man could give the devil lessons! Yet what could I do? I wanted Rachel, so I had to agree. *(Jacob)*

* * *

Leah:

Sharing a husband guarantees discontent, rivalry. I must say that Jacob did not refuse to come to my bed, and so I bore son after son for him—four of them! And with each one I kept hoping—in vain, apparently—that it would make him love me.

So far, Rachel couldn't get pregnant. She got so desperate that she gave Jacob her slave girl Bilhah as a concubine, saying, "If she gives birth on my knees, I can have my family through her." That's a custom in this area—not very fair to the slave girl. But then, not much is fair to a slave girl. I think I heard that Jacob's grandmother Sarah tried the same thing with her slave –Hagar, was it?—and what a world of trouble that caused!

But Rachel's slave Bilhah had two sons. And since I seemed to stop bearing after my four, I decided I would try it too, and gave my slave Zilpah to him. She had two sons that I named Gad (lucky) and Asher (happy). (Okay, so I wasn't fair to my slave either.)

During this period of one-upsmanship, my oldest son Reuben brought me some mandrakes he found in a field. A mandrake is a root of an herb that's shaped sort of like a man; it's been used for centuries to help a woman get pregnant. Rachel saw them and said, "Please give me some of your son's mandrakes."

The nerve of her! "Wasn't it enough that you took away my husband?" I snapped. (Since I was married to him first, I had certain marital rights, but Rachel seemed to manage who and when he slept with someone, and I was way down on the list.)

"Well, all right," she said. "Jacob can sleep with you tonight in return for your son's mandrakes."

So I met him when he came in from the fields, and told him, "You must sleep with me tonight. I have hired you with my son's mandrakes." I wonder if that made him feel like a prostitute. Well, no matter, he slept with me, and I got pregnant—son number five, Issachar, my reward.

After that I had another son and then, after my daughter Dinah was born, God remembered Rachel and she finally had a child she named Joseph. But, never satisfied, Rachel went around saying, "I wish the LORD would give me another son."   *(Leah)*

* * *

Jacob:

Leah, whatever her lack of beauty was very fertile, and altogether she gave me six sons and a daughter, and after several years, my beloved Rachel gave me one son. I also had two sons by Zilpah, Leah's handmaid and two by Bilhah, Rachel's handmaid. That was eleven sons and a daughter in the fourteen years since my marriage.

In the years we lived in Paddan Aram, I worked for Laban, but was also able to build up my own flocks. No one could accuse me of being lazy. I really worked hard to increase Laban's flocks as well as my own. But eventually feelings rode high between Laban's sons and me. They resented that my flocks increased faster than theirs, so we found it better to keep some distance between us. They seemed to think I was cheating. (Now I wonder where they would get that idea. It couldn't possibly be my name, could it?)

Twice, God had spoken to me in a dream, telling me to go back home, but I didn't go just then, even though my father must have been close to 130 years old, and no one ever knows how many more years he might have. When Joseph was born, I told Laban I wanted to go back home, but he decided I was good luck for him—well, what he actually said was the LORD had blessed him because of me. So he said, "Name your wages and I'll pay them."

What we worked out was this: my "wages" would be all the speckled, spotted, or dark-colored lambs or goats. If any un-speckled goat or light-colored lamb was found in my flocks, it would be considered stolen. He agreed. We separated the flocks, and kept them a three-day journey apart, to make sure the flocks couldn't mix.

I had come up with a complicated plan to make sure all mine would bear streaked or spotted or speckled young, just it had in a dream I'd had years ago, the first time God told me to go back to my native land. The plan seemed to work. Whether it did or not, my flocks grew strong and numerous and I was prospering in spite of Laban changing my wages over and over.

But my prosperity caused my brothers-in-law to complain that I had taken everything their father had, and that I got rich on what really belonged to Laban. Although Laban had never been real buddy-buddy before, he was definitely cooler now. It looked like it was time to head home before the sputtering family feud exploded.

When I decided to head back to Canaan, I told Rachel and Leah to meet me out in the fields where no one could overhear. I told them God had told me to go back home, but I had also noticed a definite cooling in the way their father talked to me.

"Not that I think your father would harm me—I feel that God has protected me—but it begins to seem wise to leave your father and brothers, and go back home," I said. "You brothers have become definitely unfriendly to me. I overheard them talking, and they think that I have taken everything their father owned."

They both agreed to go. They told me, "We've been cut out of his will anyway. He treats us like strangers. He sold us to you, and then he used up what you paid for us. If God has taken anything away from him, it was what really belongs to us and our children. So—do whatever God has told you to do."

And so we did.

Chapter 15. Heading Home

LEAVING LABAN

As soon as I could get things together, we left without telling anyone. My wives and the children were mounted on camels so we could make good time. I drove the flocks and other animals ahead of us, and we had our possessions in carts. Laban didn't know we had left for three days, and it took him another seven days to catch up with us. When he caught up with us, he claimed to be angry that I was "stealing his daughters, and I hadn't even let him kiss his grandchildren and daughters goodbye." As if he cared! He also let it slip that God had warned him in a dream to be careful how he spoke to me.

But what really made him angry was his household gods were missing. "Why did you steal my idols?" he yelled.

Whatever made him think I would want his idols? He knew that I, like my father and grandfather, worship the LORD, not his silly pieces of stone. (I didn't know until later that Rachel *had* stolen the gods. Possession of the idols implies headship of the family, and she was trying to guarantee my right to her father's property.)

I gave him permission to look for them, and he looked everywhere! But thanks to my clever Rachel, he couldn't find anything.

Well, I'd had enough. I just boiled over, telling him:

'What is my crime? How have I wronged you that you hunt me down? Now that you have searched through all my goods, what have you found that belongs to your household? Put it here in front of your relatives and mine, and let them judge between the two of us.

I have been with you for twenty years now. Your sheep and goats have not miscarried, nor have I eaten rams from your flocks. I did not bring you animals torn by wild beasts; I bore the loss myself. And you demanded payment for whatever was stolen by day or night. ... Twenty years I was in your household. I worked for you fourteen years for your two daughters and six years for your flocks, and you changed my wages ten times. If the God of my father, the God of Abraham and the Fear of Isaac, had not been with me, you would surely have sent me away empty-handed. But God has seen my hardship and the toil of my hands, and last night he rebuked you."   *(Genesis 31:36-42)*

We set up a witness stone pillar and a pile of rocks, called The Pile to Remind Us [Mizpah]. Laban said,

"May the LORD keep watch between you and me while we are away from each other. If you mistreat my daughters or if you take any wives besides my daughters, even though no one is with us, remember that God is a witness between you and me. ... This heap is a witness, and this pillar is a witness, that I will not go past this heap to your side to harm you and that you will not go past this heap and pillar to my side to harm me. May the God of Abraham and the God of Nahor, the God of their father, judge between us." (Genesis 31:49-53)

In other words, he was saying, Stay on your side and I'll stay on mine. And may the LORD keep his eye on you because I don't trust you as far as I could throw a camel!

And the feeling is mutual!

Well, we did end up eating a meal together, and the next morning Laban kissed his grandchildren and his daughters and blessed them. I couldn't help wondering if that was both the first and last time he showed any affection to anyone.

READY FOR ESAU

So after God had spoken to me a second time, I was heading back, knowing I would have to face Esau, but hoping that the intervening years had taken some of the sting out of the wound I had inflicted. I wasn't going to sneak back, though. I sent him a message that I was coming.

When my servants returned with the disquieting news that Esau was coming to meet me with four hundred men, my heart sank. "O God," I prayed, "you told me to return home and I have. Please deliver me from my brother's anger. You promised that you will prosper me and make my descendants as the sand of the seashore. I'm holding you to your promise."

"God helps those who help themselves" is the way I tend to think. (Wrong!) So instead of believing God's promise and trusting him to do it, I tried to plan a way to protect my family. I divided the people of my company and all the herds and flocks into two companies, hoping that at least one could escape if Esau attacked us.

In addition, I decided to send Esau a gift, a huge gift. I sorted out two hundred each of female goats, ewes, and donkeys, and twenty male goats, twenty rams, and ten male donkeys. I also set out thirty female camels with their young, forty cows and ten bulls. I divided them up according to each kind, and sent each herd individually with my servants "Keep space between them," I told the servants. "When you men with the first bunch meet Esau and he asks you who you belong to and who owns all these animals, tell him, "These are a gift from your brother Jacob to my lord Esau." I told each servant in charge of the other four groups to say the same thing. I hoped the gifts would ease Esau's anger!

Once I sent off my "Appeasement Gift" (or bribe) to Esau, I hurried to get my wives and children on the other side of the stream, and everything else I owned.

READY TO WRESTLE ?

But night fell, catching me alone on this side. In the dark, someone suddenly came upon me, and grappled with me. I couldn't tell who it was, but I had never wrestled with one so strong! I began to suspect that I was wrestling with no ordinary man. My opponent countered every move. All night we sweated, strained, tried different holds, and neither one of us would cry "I yield." Although he threw me oftener than I threw him, my stubbornness made me fight on.

It was near dawn when suddenly his hands bore down with supernatural strength and popped my hip free of its joint. "Let me go, for the dawn is breaking," he demanded.

So what? I wondered. Groaning, but gripping still with sweat-slick hands, I gasped, "Not until you bless me"—small return, indeed, for all my agony.

"What is your name?" he asked.

"Jacob, the Trickster," I panted.

And he said, "Your name will no longer be Jacob, but Israel, he who struggles with God; for you have wrestled with God and with men and have overcome."   *(Jacob)*

PENIEL

by Betty Spence

Lord, is this Your strength
leaning into mine?
Has it come to this. . .
has the God of Jacob
come to this desolate place
to wrestle
with my stubborn will?

Will You thus contend
for the mastery of my life?
Do You love me, Lord,
that much?

Then, bless me, Lord.
I won't let You go until
You bless me, Lord.
How else can one who limps
prevail?

* * *

Jacob:

I called that place Peniel [face of God] because I saw God face to face and yet my life was spared.

This wrestling match was no draw. Yes, I won a new name: Israel. But I also won a hip that warns of weather-change, and a life-long limp reminding me at every step, I can't get the best of God.

REUNION OF BROTHERS

Jacob looked up and there was Esau, coming with his four hundred men; so he divided the children among Leah, Rachel, and the two female servants. He put the female servants and their children in front, Leah and her children next, and Rachel and Joseph in the rear. He himself went on ahead and bowed down to the ground seven times as he approached his brother.   (Genesis 33:1-3)

I feared that Esau had been nursing his anger for the past twenty years, and if he was, maybe Rachel and Joseph could escape, so I put the ones I loved best at the back, the safest place. I know. It's a terrible thing for a parent to risk any of his children, but if you were in my place, how would you do it? I was still hoping that my gift (my bribe) of over five hundred animals would appease him. But even so, I meant to show him that I was coming in peace, and hoping he did too. Seven times I dropped to the ground in homage as I walked toward my brother.

The one thing I never expected to happen—happened! He ran to me, threw his arms around me, and hugged and kissed me. We both cried.

Then my brother looked up and, seeing the women and children, said, "Who are these people with you?"

As each group of women and children came forward and bowed down, I told him, "These are the children God has given me. God has been good to me, your servant."

On his way to meet me, Esau had passed the herds I had sent him. I told him they were my gift to him. He said he didn't need them and wasn't going to accept them, but I begged him, and he finally accepted the gift. (It made *me* feel better anyway.)

He also offered to come along with us, but I begged off, saying we would hold him back. My flocks with little ones, and my children, would go too slow for him and his men. He even offered to leave some of his men with us, and I politely turned down that offer too. Frankly, I still wasn't completely sure of his goodwill.

I think Esau thought we were headed for Edom where he lived. (I may have led him to think that—not lying, you know, just misdirection.) But after he left to go home, we went a different way. Living too close to each other probably would not be wise, considering our past discord.

We stopped at a place we named Succoth (meaning shelters). We named it that because I built a house for my family and shelters for my animals there. Later we moved down near the city of Shechem in Canaan. I camped east of the city, and I built an altar there and named it after God, the God of Israel.

But that area proved to be, uh, not a good place to settle down. *(Jacob)*

Chapter 16: Jacob's Children, Like Father, Like Sons

SHAME AT SHECHEM

(Jacob)

My daughter Dinah was visiting some women of the area when a young man named Shechem kidnapped and raped her. He was the son of Hamor, the ruler of the city of Shechem. He fell in love with Dinah and told his father he wanted to marry her. He was highly respected in his family, so his father came to talk with me.

But in the meantime my sons were furious at what was done to their sister, their *only* sister. They devised a horrible plan. With the excuse that "we can't give her to a man who isn't circumcised," they said that if Shechem and all the men of the city would consent to be circumcised, they would let her marry him. Not expecting treachery, the men of the city agreed to it.

Three days later, while all of them were still in pain, two of Jacob's sons, Simeon and Levi, Dinah's brothers, took their swords and attacked the unsuspecting city, killing every male.. They put Hamor and his son Shechem to the sword and took Dinah from Shechem's house and left.

The [other] *sons of Jacob came upon the dead bodies and looted the city where their sister had been defiled. They seized their flocks and herds and donkeys and everything else of theirs in the city and out in the fields. They carried off all their wealth and all their wives and children, taking as plunder everything in the houses.   (Genesis 34:25-29)*

It was a terrible thing to do. I've done many wrong things in my life, but nothing on this scale. And when I told them that their actions had put our whole family in peril and I was afraid that the local Canaanites would hate us and join forces to attack us, my sons showed neither fear nor remorse. They only said, "We will not allow our sister to be treated like a prostitute."

Well, yes, but –killing every man in the city? And looting? And carrying off all the women and children for slaves?

My sons were no more than godless barbarians! I was ashamed, ashamed of my children! Ashamed of myself that I hadn't been a better example. I had built an altar to God here, but it was evident that evil still ruled our hearts and minds. Those false gods that Rachel had stolen from her father—they had to go! *(Jacob)*

* * *

Reuben:

We are a wild bunch. I'm Reuben, oldest son of my mother Leah. As the oldest, I should have put my foot down when my brothers got out of hand, since Father didn't. There was that real bad time when Simeon and Levi, two of my full-brothers, attacked the city of Shechem because the ruler's son, also named Shechem, had raped our sister Dinah. Staying around there was a really bad idea.

Father said we brothers as well as all the servants had to give Father any foreign gods we had stashed away and the rings from our ears (I don't know why the rings, but anyway…) and Father buried them under the oak tree at Shechem. He wanted to make sure we would not be tempted to worship those false gods, I guess. For sure, after what my brothers did at Shechem, we wouldn't be going back there to dig them up.   *(Reuben)*

* * *

BACK TO BETHEL

Then God said to Jacob, "Go up to Bethel and settle there, and build an altar there to God, who appeared to you when you were fleeing from your brother Esau." (Genesis 35:1)

Jacob:

After the trouble at Shechem, we had to make a fresh start in a new place. Most important of all, we had to get right with God. I called the family together, and said: "Get rid of those false gods. We have to make a fresh start, so show your willingness by bathing and changing your clothes. We're going back to Bethel where I first met God, and I'm going to build an altar there because God helped me out of trouble more than once. You may think He isn't with us and watching, but God has been with me everywhere I went."

My family and servants brought out all their hidden false gods, and I disposed of them by burying them under the oak at Shechem where I was sure no one would dare to go back to dig them up. Then we hurried to get our things together, and left. I'm sure God had put a fear of us in the local people, because they didn't follow us to take revenge for what my sons did.

Once back at Bethel, my mother's nurse, Deborah, died. She had come with my mother from her childhood home years before. We buried her under the oak tree at Bethel, and called that place Oak of Crying.

It was while we were at Bethel, God spoke to me again, saying that I was no longer 'Jacob,' I was now 'Israel'. He confirmed the agreement he had made with me at Bethel years before, and with my father and grandfather. He said:

I am God Almighty [El Shaddai]. Be fruitful and increase in number. A nation and a community of nations will come from you, and kings will be among your descendants. The land I gave to Abraham and Isaac I also give to you, and I will give this land to your descendants after you. (Genesis 35:11,12)

After God left me, I set up a stone and poured a drink offering and olive oil on the stone. Because God had met me there in that place formerly called Luz, I named it Bethel, 'house of God.'

Eventually we moved on from Bethel but, before reaching Ephrath [Bethlehem], my beloved Rachel went into labor. Things went terribly wrong, and she died after giving birth. She knew the child was a son, and she said to name him Ben-Oni meaning Son of my Sorrow. I couldn't bear that reminder of her pain. I named him Benjamin, son of the right hand or favorite son.

Ah Rachel, my dearest love. I miss you still.

Names, names. And a new name for me. Learning to answer to Israel instead of Jacob took a while, and longer still to fit that new name. Within my breast that old name wrestles with the new. My new name is slowly shaping my nature after God's. Too slowly, I fear.

My father Isaac was staying at Mamre near Hebron where he and grandfather Abraham had lived. I went to see him, knowing the end might be near because he was very old.

When Father died at the age of one hundred eighty, I sent a messenger to my brother. Esau came from the mountains of Edom where he and his wives and children were living. Together we buried our father. Esau had been especially close to our father, so I knew this was very hard on him.

But we had too much bad history to ever have the closeness one would expect of twins. He went back to his mountains and I stayed in Canaan. Too far may be safer than too close. *(Jacob)*

Chapter 17. Joseph, Beloved, Hated

THAT DREAMER !

Now Israel loved Joseph more than any of his other sons, because he had been born to him in his old age; and he made an ornate robe for him. When his brothers saw that their father loved him more than any of them, they hated him and could not speak a kind word to him.   (Genesis 37:3,4)

Reuben:

Parents shouldn't have favorites, but Father did. And it was very clear who his favorites were: Joseph, who was next to youngest, and Benjamin, the baby. They were the children of his favorite wife Rachel who had died in childbirth with Benjamin.

Father had a richly ornamented robe made for Joseph and he flaunted it. And then, making it worse, Joseph began to have these "dreams," so he said. In one dream we were all binding sheaves in the field, and all of our sheaves bowed down to his. In another dream, the sun and moon and eleven stars bowed down to him. That one even bothered Father who rebuked him, saying, "Will your mother and I and your brothers actually come and bow down to you?"

Carrying tales about his brothers, especially Bilhah's and Zilpah's sons, didn't improve relationships. He told Father they were lazy or not doing the job right. So who made *him* boss?

As you can see, things were not all sweetness and light in our family of brothers. So that day when Father sent him to check on us as we cared for the flocks, anger had built up to the danger point. We saw him coming in the distance—that fancy robe was unmistakable—and some of my brothers decided to get rid of "that dream expert" as they called him. They actually planned to kill him and say a wild animal had killed him.

When I heard their plans, I knew that, being the oldest, I couldn't let them kill their own brother. I quickly suggested that instead of shedding his blood, we just throw him into this nearby dry cistern. I had a half-baked plan to rescue him secretly and take him back to Father. My brothers accepted my idea of throwing him into the cistern. When he came up to us, they stripped him of that robe (which we all hated) and threw him in.

I had to go off somewhere to tend to a sheep in distress, but I had every intention of rescuing him. They were eating lunch when I left, and I thought I could rescue him later. But while I was away, a caravan of Ishamelite merchants came by, headed down to Egypt.

I was told later that Judah came up with the idea to sell him to the slave traders rather than kill him, and they all agreed. No blood would be on their hands, that way. *(Reuben)*

* * *

UNFAIR EXCHANGE

Rich fragrance drifts
from camel-loads of spice and myrrh
and mingles with the reek
of sweat and sheep.
We haggle with the slavers
while harness bells chime counterpoint
to Joseph's piteous pleas.
A bargain struck—
that Dreamer sold—
we take their silver coins,
and then concoct
a tale for Jacob's ears.

So! Twenty shekels for ten men—
that's two apiece.

My two seem stained.
Could that be ... blood?

* * *

Reuben:

When I came back and found Joseph was gone, I tore my clothes. "What have you done with him?" I yelled.

"Rather than kill him, we sold him to the Ishmaelites. We got twenty shekels for him. Here's your share," Levi said.

I threw the shekels on the ground. "How could you do this? Sell your own brother to the slavers!"

"Hey, he's out of our hair—permanently—and it would have been a sin to kill him, wouldn't it?"

As if that worried him! My brothers Simeon and Levi didn't seem to go by the same rules as most people.

As for the rest of my brothers? Their bright idea was to kill a goat and dip that despised coat in it and tell Father we found it like that. Don't tell him what we did, just let him assume that Joseph was dead and killed by a wild animal.

As Father mourned for Joseph, we tried to comfort him. But our guilt gnawed at us. After all, we had hated our brother, plotted to kill him, sold him into lifelong slavery. Father's sorrow, like our sin, weighed heavy.   *(Reuben)*

* * *

JOSEPH IN CHAINS, JOSEPH IN TROUBLE

Now Joseph had been taken down to Egypt. Potiphar, an Egyptian who was one of Pharaoh's officials, the captain of the guard, bought him from the Ishmaelites who had taken him there.

The LORD was with Joseph so that he prospered, and he lived in the house of his Egyptian master. When his master saw that the LORD was with him and that the LORD gave him success in everything he did, Joseph found favor in his eyes and became his attendant.

Potiphar put him in charge of his household, and he entrusted to his care everything he owned. From the time he put him in charge of his household and of all that he owned, the LORD blessed the household of the Egyptian because of Joseph. ... So Potiphar left everything he had in Joseph's care; with Joseph in charge, he did not concern himself with anything except the food he ate.

Now Joseph was well-built and handsome, and after a while his master's wife took notice of Joseph and said, "Come to bed with me!" (Genesis 39:1-7)

* * *

Handmaid:

I always say no one knows a woman better than her personal handmaid. Not even her husband. In fact, certainly not her husband.

My master Potiphar, as captain of the guard and one of Pharaoh's officials, has a high ranking position, and he also has a high-ranking wife—her father was very high in the king's regard. As her personal handmaid, I bathe her, dress her, see her without her makeup, see when she frowns at the mirror. I know her opinion of her friends and her obsession with new clothes. I know she is determined to get her own way no matter what. I also know she has a roving eye.

At first sight, that Hebrew slave the master brought home looked really scruffy, not clean-shaven like our Egyptian men. But Yusef (as we called him) certainly cleaned up well. So of course my mistress noticed, especially after Master Potiphar put him in charge of the household. Yusef was very efficient, conscientious, and kind to us other servants.

It wasn't long before I noticed the mistress had her eye on him. I'd seen her in action before, but never in her own household. She made his life difficult, touching his hand when he held the door open for her. I'll say this for him, he showed no improper interest in her, however, and he always tried to make sure there were other servants around when she came in the same room. That only made my mistress more obsessed with him. But none of us servants were in the house that day because she had sent us out on some pretext.

She tried to seduce him, but he would have none of it. I soon heard what happened, because when I got back she was having a full-blown temper tantrum. I tried to calm her down but she was screaming, "I hate him! I hate him. He wouldn't have anything to do with me! You know what that stupid slave had the nerve to tell me? 'My master has withheld nothing from me except you, because you are his wife. How could I do such a wicked thing and sin against my God!' Nobody, *nobody* treats me like that and gets away with it!"

And then she suddenly turned quiet, and said viciously, "But I grabbed his cloak as he ran! I'll make him sorry! I'll show Potiphar his cloak and claim he tried to rape me when no one was in the house. Potiphar will have him killed. That will teach him what his foolish religious scruples can bring down on his head. Potiphar will kill him, and good riddance!"

And she tried. She lied about him to Potiphar. But Potiphar didn't kill Yusef. He could have, and he was angry—more at his wife than Yusef, I suspect. I'm sure he wasn't fooled by his wife's lies and tears, but he had to do something to placate her. As captain of the king's guard, Potiphar is in charge of the prison where the king's prisoners are kept. So instead of having Yusef killed as she demanded, he sent Yusef to the prison.

Poor Yusef. He is such a good man. I hope he is all right.

But my mistress is even worse to deal with, now. Being her personal maid is not the easy task I expected when I first started here. I wish I could get out of this situation. I wouldn't mind being sold— or anything! Anything, just so I wouldn't have to deal with her any more.   *(Handmaid)*

* * *

IN CHARGE OF PRISON and
DREAM INTERPRETATION

But while Joseph was there in the prison, the LORD was with him; he showed him kindness and granted him favor in the eyes of the prison warden. So the warden put Joseph in charge of all those held in the prison, and he was made responsible for all that was done there. The warden paid no attention to anything under Joseph's care, because the LORD was with Joseph and gave him success in whatever he did.   (Genesis 39:21-23)

* * *

Cupbearer:

As the king's cupbearer, I had a most prestigious position in Pharaoh's court. My job was to bring him wine in his own cup, and then taste it before giving it to him, thus proving it had not been poisoned. You could say that the king's life rested in my hands.

The chief baker for the court was my friend, and we were both proud of our responsible positions. But one day, out of the blue, the king decided that both of us had offended him, and had us put in prison, the same place where Joseph was confined. The captain of the guard (I think he was named Potiphar) assigned us to Joseph who was in charge of everything even though technically he was a prisoner too.

After some time, each of us—the baker and I—had a dream the same night. It seemed that the dreams had important meanings but we had no one to interpret them. When Joseph came to our cell the next morning, he noticed we looked dejected, and asked why. We told him that we had each had a dream that seemed to have a meaning. He said that interpretations of dreams belonged to God, but he asked us to tell him our dreams. Maybe he could help.

As he heard my dream, he said it meant that I would be restored to my positon in three days. I was thrilled. Joseph asked me to remember him and mention him to Pharaoh since he was unjustly imprisoned.

Unfortunately the dream of my friend the baker had a horrible meaning. In three days he would be killed, impaled!

Three days later was the king's birthday. I was restored to my position, but just as Joseph said, the baker was killed. I am ashamed to confess that I forgot my promise to remember Joseph and how he interpreted my dream.

In fact, I forgot him for two full years, until the time when Pharaoh had a dream about seven sleek and healthy cows and seven gaunt ones that ate up the sleek ones. Then that same night he had a second dream about seven healthy heads of grain followed by seven skinny heads of grain. When he sent for all the wise men and magicians, not one could tell him what it meant.

Suddenly I remembered Joseph. "Today I am reminded of my shortcomings," I said, shame-faced. And I told them of the dreams Joseph had correctly interpreted for me and the chief baker. Pharaoh promptly sent for Joseph.

As soon as Joseph was shaved and changed his clothes, he was brought before the king. When Pharaoh told him he had heard that Joseph could interpret dreams, Joseph looked over at me and nodded in recognition. (I vowed I would make a special effort to apologize as soon as possible.)

Then Joseph told Pharaoh –just as he had previously told the baker and me—that he himself couldn't interpret the dreams but God would give Pharaoh the answer. *(Cupbearer)*

* * *

Then Joseph said to Pharaoh, "The dreams of Pharaoh are one and the same. God has revealed to Pharaoh what he is about to do. The seven good cows are seven years... The seven lean, ugly cows are seven years of famine. ... Seven years of great abundance are coming throughout the land of Egypt, but seven years of famine will follow them. Then all the abundance in Egypt will be forgotten, and the famine will ravage the land. ...

"And now let Pharaoh look for a discerning and wise man and put him in charge of the land of Egypt. Let Pharaoh appoint commissioners over the land to take a fifth of the harvest of Egypt during the seven years of abundance. They should collect all the food of these good years that are coming and store up the grain under the authority of Pharaoh, to be kept in the cities for food. This food should be held in reserve for the country, to be used during the seven years of famine ... so that the country may not be ruined by the famine."

The plan seemed good to Pharaoh and to all his officials. So Pharaoh asked them, "Can we find anyone like this man, one in whom is the spirit of God?"
(Genesis 41:25-27, 30, 33-38)

Chapter 18. JOSEPH IN CHARGE

NUMBER 2 MAN IN EGYPT

Then Pharaoh said to Joseph, "Since God has made all this known to you, there is no one so discerning and wise as you. You shall be in charge of my palace, and all my people are to submit to your orders. Only with respect to the throne will I be greater than you."

So Pharaoh said to Joseph, "I hereby put you in charge of the whole land of Egypt." Then Pharaoh took his signet ring from his finger and put it on Joseph's finger. He dressed him in robes of fine linen and put a gold chain around his neck. He had him ride in a chariot as his second-in-command, and people shouted before him, "Make way!" Thus he put him in charge of the whole land of Egypt.

(Genesis 41:39-43)

* * *

Joseph:

From prison to palace. Whoever would have imagined such a thing? Back when I was a child in my mother's tent I wondered if my dreams had importance, but when all of my family including my father thought I was being ridiculous, I tried to put those childish ideas out of my head. Forgot them, so I thought. Especially when I ended up roped together with other slaves and dragged up and down hills and over deserts on the way to an Egypt slave market.

It was a long fall from being the favored son dressed in an elegant robe, to a slave standing naked on the slave block where I was an item for sale, just like a horse or a basket of vegetables. I struggled not to show my anger or humiliation as I was poked by prospective buyers to see how healthy I was, did I have all my teeth, if I was castrated or circumcised. They talked about me as if I were a donkey instead of a human being. Of course, I was at a disadvantage, knowing next to no Egyptian. Out of necessity, I had to learn the language quickly.

When Potiphar bought me, I determined that I would become the best slave he had ever owned. He proved to be a good master, and when I proved useful to him, he gave me more and more opportunities to develop the abilities I began to see as God-given.

Of course, that problem with his wife put an abrupt end to my time there. I swore to him that I had not tried to rape his wife, and I think he believed me, but he couldn't ignore the situation. Because of her family's prominence, he had to do something. So I ended up in the prison that he was in charge of. I'm sure Potiphar arranged that—and I am positive that *God* planned it!

I was able to use my abilities there in his prison as I had in his house. I wouldn't be surprised to find that Potiphar was behind my advancement in the prison—after all, he was the boss. But I determined that wherever I was, I would do my very best. I was sure that God would use me and bless the work of my hands.

I was seventeen when sold, and I had thirteen years of ups and downs before Pharaoh made me his vizier, the second-in-charge man after Pharaoh. He put me in charge of his palace, in charge of all Egypt, and in charge of the Famine Relief program that I had suggested.

NEW NAME, NEW FAMILY

Pharaoh gave me a new name: Zaphenath-Paneah. After all, the second man in Egypt couldn't have a Hebrew name; he had to have an Egyptian name.

He also gave me lovely Asenath as my wife. Her father is Potiphera, a priest of Heliopolis. With that connection, I was later able to make things easier on all the priests during the years of famine. Asenath gave me two sons, both born before the Years of Famine.

My first son I named Manasseh, which sounds like the Hebrew word for "forget." I chose that for several reasons. I was sure I had been forgotten by my brothers who wanted to get rid of me—and they did a good job of that! Forgotten by the king's cupbearer for two years. That was not easy to accept, but God had his plan even there. But mainly I chose Manasseh as my son's name because God had made *me* forget all my trouble and all my father's household. When Manasseh was born I realized I had achieved peace: peace with my past, peace in my new life.

My second son I named Ephraim which, in Hebrew, sounds like "twice fruitful." I now had a family that loved me, in place of one that hated me. Truly, I was doubly blessed—two sons where it looked like I would be a slave to my dying day, and never have children. Yes, God blessed me by making me fruitful, doubly fruitful—in the land of my suffering. Whereas Manasseh reminds me I had found peace with my past, Ephraim reminds that, by God's grace, I was now in the place of plenty, of fruitfulness. And those first seven years were unbelievably fruitful all throughout Egypt.

I was busy those seven years of plenty, traveling up and down Egypt, building granaries, and getting huge quantities of grain stored up in each city against the seven bad years to come. We actually stored up such tremendous quantities of grain that I stopped keeping records. It was almost beyond counting. But we were ready when the bountiful years turned to years of famine.

(Joseph)

* * *

The seven years of abundance in Egypt came to an end, and the seven years of famine began, just as Joseph had said. There was famine in all the other lands, but in the whole land of Egypt there was food. When all Egypt began to feel the famine, the people cried to Pharaoh for food. Then Pharaoh told all the Egyptians, "Go to Joseph and do what he tells you." ... (Genesis 41:53-55)

Chapter 19. Dreams Come True

THE HUNGER YEARS

When the famine had spread over the whole country, Joseph opened all the storehouses and sold grain to the Egyptians, for the famine was severe throughout Egypt. And all the world came to Egypt to buy grain from Joseph, because the famine was severe everywhere. (Genesis 41:56,57)

* * *

Farmer in Canaan:

Egypt is not the only land where famine stalked. When crops fail, not just one year, but year after year, everything hurts—our families, our animals.

Both the early and late rains failed. We need them to sprout the seed, make it grow, ripen the grain and the fruit trees. With no rain there's no grass for the livestock. It breaks your heart to see your starving animals wander over the brown, dried-up fields, looking for a mouthful of grass, a swallow of water.

In winter we generally look up at the eternal snows of Mount Hermon, but now even Mount Hermon is mostly bare. Without snow-melt to fill them, streams are mere trickles even in the spring and completely dry by summer.

We farmers know we have to put aside part of this year's harvest so we can have seed to plant next year. There's a saying: "Eat seed-corn this year, starve next year." Yet how long can you resist eating it when your stomach aches, you grow weaker every day, and your starving children beg you for something to eat? The mother of your newborn finds her milk dries up, and the hungry baby whimpers, no longer strong enough for a full-throated cry.

And then you hear a rumor.

They say that Egypt has food—for a price. *(Farmer)*

* * *

JACOB: 'GO TO EGYPT FOR FOOD'

When Jacob learned that there was grain in Egypt, he said to his sons, ... "I have heard that there is grain in Egypt. Go down there and buy some for us, so that we may live and not die."

Then ten of Joseph's brothers went down to buy grain from Egypt. But Jacob did not send Benjamin, Joseph's brother, with the others, because he was afraid that harm might come to him. So Israel's sons were among those who went to buy grain, for there was famine in the land of Canaan also.

Now Joseph was the governor of the land, the person who sold grain to all its people. (Genesis 42:1-6)

Joseph:

How my heart leaped when I saw them. It had been twenty years since I had seen these brothers of mine, flesh of my flesh. As I looked in each familiar face, I saw all were here but one, my full-brother Benjamin. I wondered, had he died of starvation as so many have? How could I find out if Benjamin and my father still lived without letting them know who I was?

So when Joseph's brothers arrived, they bowed down to him with their faces to the ground. As soon as Joseph saw his brothers, he recognized them, but he pretended to be a stranger and spoke harshly to them. "Where do you come from?" he asked. ... Although Joseph recognized his brothers, they did not recognize him. Then he remembered his dreams about them. (Genesis 42:6-9)

It's not surprising that they did not recognize me. No one could have imagined that the second man in Egypt was the brother they had sold twenty years ago. To them I was an Egyptian in dress and speech, for I spoke to them through an interpreter.

God had made such a change in my life, in my heart. But had he worked in theirs in these twenty years?

He said to them, "You are spies! You have come to see where our land is unprotected."

"No, my lord," they answered. "Your servants have come to buy food. We are all the sons of one man. Your servants are honest men, not spies. ... Your servants were twelve brothers, the sons of one man, who lives in the land of Canaan. The youngest is now with our father, and one is no more."

Joseph said to them, "It is just as I told you: You are spies! And this is how you will be tested: As surely as Pharaoh lives, you will not leave this place unless your youngest brother comes here. Send one of your number to get your brother; the rest of you will be kept in prison, so that your words may be tested to see if you are telling the truth. If you are not, then as surely as Pharaoh lives, you are spies!" And he put them all in custody for three days. (Genesis 42: 9-17)

Of course my brothers had no idea I could understand them, but by accusing them of spying, I put them off-balance. As they tried to convince this haughty Egyptian, the only one who could provide their desperately needed food, they blurted out exactly what I wanted to know. My father still lived, and so did my young brother Benjamin.

But I needed to know other things too. Did they hate Benjamin as they had hated me? To what extent would they go to protect him if he was threatened? After all, they would have killed me. Maybe they would be as willing to throw Benjamin to the slavers as they had me.

So I put them in prison and let them "stew" for three days. Let them have a tiny taste of what I had experienced—imprisoned, uncertain what might happen, surrounded by criminals whose language they did not know. I knew what months of it had done to me. I had been driven to my knees before Yahweh as well as before the other prisoners.

JOSEPH TESTS HIS BROTHERS

In those three days I devised a plan to find out what was really in their hearts. I called them before me, and said (still through the interpreter), "Do this and you will live, for I fear God." Telling them I feared God should assure them that they wouldn't be killed out of hand—maybe. So I presented another option for them to prove they were not spies. "You tell me you are honest men. If you want to convince me, you will leave one of your brothers behind, to stay here in prison while the rest of you go back with grain for your starving households."

They didn't know whether to be happy because of the food or still worried about leaving someone behind as hostage. To keep up the pressure on them, I ordered, "You must bring your youngest brother to me, so that your words may be verified and that the brother left behind may not die."

Hearing them tell each other that they knew this was punishment for their heartless actions to me, years ago —well, I could hardly maintain my stern face. And when Reuben said to the others, "Didn't I tell you not to sin against the boy?" I had to turn away and hide my tears.

But I had started this, and I needed to carry it through, so I pointed out Simeon—I knew him to be a cruel man who had killed without remorse—and had him bound while they watched. He deserved a taste of prison; maybe it would do him good.

Then I gave orders to fill their grain bags and give them provisions for their journey. Secretly, however, I ordered that each man's silver be returned to the grain sacks.   (Joseph)

* * *

They loaded their grain on their donkeys and left. At the place where they stopped for the night, one of them opened his sack to get feed for his donkey, and he saw his silver in the mouth of his sack. "My silver has been returned," he said to his brothers. "Here it is in my sack." (Genesis 42:26-28)

Reuben:
When my brother found the silver in his sack, our hearts sank. "What has God done to us?" Judah moaned. "Now the Egyptian will be sure we are spies or thieves, and our brother will be killed."

We didn't know what to do. Return to Egypt and try to explain? We'd probably all end up in prison—after all, who would believe such a story? But our families at home were on the verge of starvation, and these bags of grain were desperately needed. We stood there, distressed, unsure. Which way to go? Home? Back to Egypt?

But the facts were plain: our donkeys were loaded with grain which we had paid for in good faith, and our hearts told us we had to go home so our families won't starve. We would take the grain to our families. Later we would do what we had to, in order to make things right. For now, the final decision was: we had to go home and tell Father.

With fearful hearts we turned our faces toward Canaan and the terrible news we had for our father. Recalling how Father had mourned when we let him think Joseph was dead, we dreaded laying this new sorrow at his feet. He was old, and this might be too much to bear, a final blow to his heart.

Then, when we got home and unloaded the grain, we found that *every one* of our sacks contained the money we had paid. With that situation along with the Egyptian demanding to see our youngest brother, Father was devastated, saying, "You are robbing me of all my children. Joseph is gone, Simeon is gone, and now you want to take Benjamin away too. Everything is against me!" And the painful thing was that he was more right than he knew. We *were* responsible for Joseph being gone.

But there was no help for it. To get Simeon back we had to take Benjamin down to Egypt when we returned. And return we must. The grain we had brought home would not last long, nor was there anywhere else to get food. Also, we had to return the silver and demonstrate that we were honest men.

In a way I still felt guilty for not rescuing Joseph twenty years before. Yes, I had to go tend to a sheep in distress, but I keep thinking I should have rushed back to my brothers when I saw the caravan of Ishmaelite merchants in the distance. Foolish regret, maybe. I never dreamed what they would do, but if I had been there.... Oh well. The world's most useless word is "if."

It was those dregs of guilt that made me tell Father, "We have to take him or you will have another lost son. Entrust Benjamin to my care. I promise, I will bring him back. You have my word, Father. If I do not bring Benjamin back to you, you may put both of my sons to death."

But Father was nothing if not stubborn. "My son will not go down there with you. I have lost his mother and his brother, and Benjamin is the only one I have left."

I bit my tongue at this statement. Jacob had ten sons beside Benjamin, and each of us—Benjamin as well—had sons and daughters! It wasn't true that Benjamin was the only one left. There was at least seventy of us. Yet it had always been painfully obvious that we six sons of Leah and the four born to his two concubines were less to him than Rachel and her two. Why couldn't our father see that?

That favoritism was the root of the awful thing done to Joseph.

He limped back to his seat. "No, he can't go. If harm should come to him, you would bring my gray head down to the grave in sorrow." It seems that we sons of Jacob are certainly good at one thing — bringing sorrow to our father. *(Reuben)*

Chapter 20. "Go Back to Egypt"

WHAT MUST BE, MUST BE

Now the famine was still severe in the land. So when they had eaten all the grain they had brought from Egypt, their father said to them, "Go back and buy us a little more food." (Genesis 43:1,2)

Judah:

When Father said that, I looked at Reuben, surprised. Had he forgotten there was a big problem in going back to Egypt? Reuben shrugged, and said, "You deal with it this time, Judah. I've done my best."

So I said to Father, "That man in Egypt warned us solemnly, 'You will not see my face again unless your brother is with you.' Don't you remember? We can only go if we take Benjamin. If you send him with us, we can go down and buy food for all of us. But if you won't send him, we can't go. That man said we will not see his face unless our brother is with us."

I guess Father had forgotten, or maybe wanted to forget. But suddenly it was my fault for telling the man we had another brother. "Why did you pull trouble down on me by telling the man you had another brother?" he snapped.

Striving for patience, I explained, "The man asked us if our father was still living, and if we had other brothers at home. It seemed a bit odd that he would ask complete strangers about these things, but we just answered his questions. How should we know he would demand to see our brother?"

I could see that Father was getting upset again. But then, lately he was more easily angered, a bit forgetful, and weakened—much to his dismay. It's true we were all constantly hungry, which didn't help anybody's disposition.

I thought I'd push this along so we could get on the road to Egypt for more food, so I said, "Send him along with me and we will go at once. At this rate, we'll all be starving soon. I myself will guarantee Benjamin's safety, and you can hold me personally responsible. If I don't bring him back and set him here in front of you in your tent, I will bear the blame all my life."

I know I should not have said it, but I was tired of the delay and of being hungry all the time, so I grumbled, "If we hadn't been dragging our feet on this, we could have gone and come back twice!"

Then Jacob showed he was still The Man, the one in charge here. He said, "If it must be, then here's what you do. Take that man a gift of our local specialties: balm and myrrh, some honey and spices, pistachios and almonds. Then take double the silver, because you have to return the silver put in your sacks by mistake. Take your brother Benjamin and go back to the man at once."

Then Father stood up, leaned on his staff as he did when he was saying something important or when talking to his God. He turned his face toward heaven, closed his eyes, and prayed, "Oh God Almighty, grant mercy to my sons before that man so he will let Simeon and Benjamin come back home. As for me, Lord, if I am to be bereaved further, so be it."

We did as Father commanded, and within a day or two we were on our way to Egypt. *(Judah)*

BACK TO EGYPT

Benjamin:

I had heard the arguments between my father and my brothers, and it all seemed to swirl about me. My brothers insisted that I had to go down to Egypt because the man down there demanded my presence or we couldn't buy any more grain. My father insisted that he refused to lose any more sons, and I was not going. Yes, he must go. No, I won't let him. Yes. No. And so the argument raged on and on.

No one seemed to think I had any say even though it was my life they argued about. But the deciding vote was cast by the dwindling food supply. An empty stomach is louder than fears of "what might happen."

My father hugged me, tears flowing down into his beard, and prayed over me that God would bring me back safe and sound. And then we ten brothers, plus a few servants, set out for Egypt.

My brothers had told me what we would see. As we traveled the desert on the way down to Egypt, all along the road we saw victims of the famine, dead animals, and sometimes dead people too. Birds of prey fought over the animals, to get what little flesh was still on the bones. I even saw men beat off the birds to get for themselves scraps to eat.

We set a watch each night; otherwise we might "wake up with our throat slit," as one of my brothers put it. Groups of unwary travelers had been attacked in the dark and killed for their food supplies.

We traveled from one waterhole to the next, making sure our water-skins and jars were filled in case the next oasis would prove to be dry. And that did happen more than once. It is scary to cross dry stream beds or reach a dry oasis, and wonder if we have enough water to keep us and our donkeys going until the next water source.

When we entered Egypt it wasn't hard to find the place where grain was being sold. The whole world seemed to be headed there. I saw men whose clothes and skin colors indicated they had traveled far. Some who had already bought what their shrinking purses could afford carried filled bags on their backs. Others had brought camels to carry the grain home, or donkeys, as we did, or other beasts of burden. Grain had to be shared between the beasts and their families. Hard decisions to make.

As at home, there were no fat people to be seen anywhere. In time of famine, to be fat is dangerous. Anyone still fat was despised since it was clear that they were eating precious food that others were literally dying for. They might be followed home and relieved of their abundance. Hunger could, and often did, over-rule any notions of fairness to one's fellowman. And of course, after two years of famine, the weakest had died. Many newborns never survived past their first months.

SUMMONED

I was so engrossed in looking around that I hardly noticed when an Egyptian came up to us and said we were required to follow him. I looked at my brothers who had obediently fallen into line to follow him. "What's going on?" I asked. "Who is he?"

"We have to follow this man," Reuben said. "He's the steward of the man in charge of selling grain. I hope we will be able to meet Simeon there. But it worries me that we have to go to his house. After all, the man accused us of being spies, last time."

Levi said, "It's about the silver we found in our sacks. I bet he plans to overpower us and seize us as slaves and take our donkeys." I wasn't overly fond of Levi, and it struck me that was just the kind of idea we could expect from him. He always expected someone to cheat or harm him, probably because those thoughts lingered in his own heart. I knew of some of the awful things he had done in the past, so I wouldn't be surprised at anything he would do.

When we reached the house, not knowing what might befall us there, Reuben put his hand on the man's arm and stopped him. "I beg your pardon, my lord. If this is about the silver we found in our sacks the last time we were here, we have brought it back and we have additional silver to pay for what we hope to get this time. We have no idea how that silver got in our sacks."

The steward looked at my brother, and with a half-smile he said an amazing thing: "It's all right. Don't be afraid. Your God, the God of your father, has given you treasure in your sacks. I received your silver. Wait here a minute."

He opened the door and went inside, as a storm of questions burst from our lips. *What did he mean? God provided that money? It doesn't make sense. And he's an Egyptian. How does he know about the God of our father?*

OUR BROTHER, RETURNED

Then the door opened and the man came out with our brother Simeon. If we were astonished before, this just capped it all! But in the hubbub, the steward raised his voice. "Come in, come in. You are welcome here."

With Simeon in the midst—I reached out and touched him to be sure it was him and not a mirage—we entered the Egyptian's beautiful house. Like honored guests, we had our feet washed, our donkeys cared for. And while we waited—because we were told that the master of the house would return home at noon—we set out the gifts we had brought. *(Benjamin)*

* * *

JOSEPH'S DINNER PARTY

Joseph:

I had seen them when they came before me but I didn't say a word to them. I couldn't count on maintaining my self-control in public. I sent them to my own house and gave my steward instructions for a big meal for them, and special instructions how they should be seated. I also told him not to explain anything about the mysterious silver. It wouldn't hurt them to work up more than a little anxiety.

But my steward was told to treat them like honored guests. According to my instructions, he brought Simeon out to them, and in general treated them politely—which made them even more nervous. I am sure that all the exaggerated rumors they had heard about Egyptians over the years only increased their fears. *Why would he treat us like this? What is he going to do to us?*

When I came home for the noon meal, I had them brought before me. I greeted them politely, accepted the gifts they had brought, and asked about their aged father. When they bowed to the floor before me, I couldn't help remembering my boyhood dream where they bowed low to me.

But it came close to breaking me up when I saw Benjamin. "Is this your youngest brother?" I asked. Then I said, "God be gracious to you, my son." But I couldn't contain my tears, and I hastily left the room to find a place where I could weep in privacy. The young boy I had last seen was now a strong, handsome man. If he had married at the age my other brothers wed, he probably had several children by now.

After getting myself under control, I washed the tears away and returned to the dining area. "Serve the meal," I commanded. I sat apart from them because Egyptians would never sit at the same table to eat with Hebrews. However, they were served from my table as a mark of honor, although they may not have known it for what it was.

I watched them from the corner of my eye, and I hid my amusement when they suddenly realized that they were seated in order, from the firstborn to the youngest. The confusion on their faces as they saw this was a secret pleasure to me. I could see them whispering to each other, probably saying, "How did anyone know our ages, to seat us this way?"

As they were served from my table, I had instructed that Benjamin's portion be five times that of anyone else. I watched carefully to see whether this was noticed, and particularly if it was a cause for resentment against Benjamin. I hoped to find out if they felt about my brother as they had felt about me. Of course, it was more likely that my own actions back then had intensified their dislike into hatred. I certainly was not completely innocent.

However, the obvious favoritism didn't seem to make any difference to their regard for Benjamin. I was glad. In fact, when one of them noticed the large helpings piling up at Benjamin's plate, they joked about how he would soon be bigger around than Reuben if he ate it all. There seemed to be a camaraderie between my young brother and all the others, and it pleased me greatly.

The excellent meal was followed by plenty of wine. And I invited them to stay overnight at my house. But in the meantime I had set up yet another test.

JOSEPH'S SECOND TEST

I wanted to be absolutely sure that my brothers did not hold the least hint of bitterness against my mother's son, Benjamin, certainly not the lethal resentment they had held against me. So I set up a second test: What would they do if he —or they themselves—were in danger of being forced into slavery? Since they had sold *me* into slavery, it seemed a splendidly ironic test.

Let the games begin.   (*Joseph*)

* * *

Now Joseph gave these instructions to the steward of his house: "Fill the men's sacks with as much food as they can carry, and put each man's silver in the mouth of his sack. Then put my cup, the silver one, in the mouth of the youngest one's sack, along with the silver for his grain." And he did as Joseph said.

As morning dawned, the men were sent on their way with their donkeys. They had not gone far from the city when Joseph said to his steward, "Go after those men at once, and when you catch up with them, say to them, 'Why have you repaid good with evil? Isn't this the cup my master drinks from and also uses for divination?* This is a wicked thing you have done.'"

When he caught up with them, he repeated these words to them. But they said to him, "Why does my lord say such things? Far be it from your servants to do anything like that! We even brought back to you from the land of Canaan the silver we found inside the mouths of our sacks. So why would we steal silver or gold from your master's house? If any of your servants is found to have it, he will die; and the rest of us will be my lord's slaves."

"Very well," he said, "let it be as you say. Whoever is found to have it will become my slave; the rest of you will be free of blame." (Genesis 44:1-10)
* divination: explaining dreams

Judah:

Sure that we were unjustly accused, and angered at the accusation, we quickly opened our sacks. The steward began an examination, beginning with Reuben, the oldest, and proceeding in order of age. Even in that fearful situation, the question buzzed in my brain: *He's doing this in the order of our birth! How can he know that? This is crazy.*

But when the cup was found in Benjamin's sack, we all tore our clothes in despair. As we reloaded the donkeys and returned to the city, I went over it again and again. *There was no way Benjamin could have taken the cup. None of us were at table with that man, so we couldn't have taken it. Had one of the other servants put it in his sack? But why would they? Nothing, absolutely nothing has made sense about this trip!*

And then my conscience began to poke at me. *Are we being punished for what we did to Joseph? He wept, begged for mercy, and we hardened our hearts against him. Oh God, You have uncovered our sin, and now we are helpless before You and before this man who thinks we have stolen from him.*

When we got back to the house, the man confronted us, saying, "What have you done? Don't you know a man like me can find things out by divination?"

"What can we say?" I asked him. "How can we prove our innocence in this? Although we are innocent of this, God has used it to uncover our former sins. We are all your slaves, we and the one who was found to have the cup."

But he would not accept that. "No. Only the man with my cup will become my slave. The rest, go back to your father in peace."

In desperation, I began to tell him the full story, from when he first inquired about our father and whether we had a younger brother. I told him about my father's fear of losing his youngest son, and how he only gave in and let Benjamin come with us because the famine was still so great back home, and we would not have survived much longer.

Then I told him that I had personally guaranteed Benjamin's return, by saying, "If I do not bring him back to you, I will bear the blame before you, my father, all my life!"

"So, please, my lord," I said. "Let me take his place, remain here as your slave, and let him return with his brothers to our father. How can I go back to my father if the lad is not with me? No! I can't bear to bring more misery down on my father's head. Take me in his place, I beg of you." *(Judah)*

Chapter 21. Revelation and Reunion

"I AM JOSEPH!"

"How can I go back to my father if the boy is not with me? No! Do not let me see the misery that would come on my father." (Genesis 44:34)

Joseph:

I thought my heart would break as I saw Judah's genuine sorrow and concern for his young brother and his aged father. I sent all my attendants out of the room. When we were alone, then I told my brothers, "I am Joseph!" The misery I had stored up for twenty years burst forth in weeping so loud that all in the house could hear me.

My brothers were speechless, terrified. And I had to reassure them. "Come close," I said. "I truly am Joseph, your brother, the one you sold into Egypt! But do not be distressed, nor angry with yourselves for selling me. God sent me ahead of you to save lives, your lives and others of our people. A remnant to be saved. It was not you who sent me here, but God."

I told them my plan of moving the whole family to Egypt in the region of Goshen which is near me. And I told them that I am planning to provide for them.

It was a time of loud weeping as we got things straightened out between us, and of joyful embraces.

The news of my brothers' arrival was told to Pharaoh, and he was pleased for me. In fact, he ordered, "Bring your father and your families back. I will give you the best of the land of Egypt." Then he had some practical suggestions about giving them wagons to move down. "Don't bother with your belongings," he said, "because the best of all Egypt will be yours."

Pharaoh extended his appreciation for my service to all of my family, giving them gifts and provisions for their journey back to Egypt.

My brothers left to go home to Canaan and bring back all their families and possessions. Knowing their characters, I couldn't resist one small jab. "Don't quarrel on the way!" I said.   *(Joseph)*

* * *

So they went up out of Egypt and came to their father Jacob in the land of Canaan. They told him, "Joseph is still alive! In fact, he is ruler of all Egypt." Jacob was stunned; he did not believe them. But when they told him everything Joseph had said to them, and when he saw the carts Joseph had sent to carry him back, the spirit of their father Jacob revived. And Israel [Jacob] said, "I'm convinced! My son Joseph is still alive. I will go and see him before I die."
(Genesis 45:25-28;)

* * *

JACOB MOVES TO EGYPT

Jacob:

It was like a dream. My sons told me Joseph was alive, but I thought I was dreaming. Many times over the years I had dreamed: *Joseph isn't really dead. He can't be.* Yet I always awoke to the reality that he was gone.

But now my sons were insisting, yes, Joseph is alive. And not only alive but the ruler of all Egypt. I was sure either they were crazy or I was.

But when they insisted, and I saw the carts Joseph had sent to carry all of us and our livestock down to Egypt, I had to believe. Opening my mind to that impossibility seemed to send a shock of energy through this old body. My spirit, long weighed down by sorrow, revived. My son Joseph is alive! And I will go and see him before I die!

We old men cling to the familiar, the places of our childhood and youth and young manhood. It's like we have grown into and become physically part of these places. To move seems to rip away part of us. Often, only dire necessity can pull us away. Over the years dire necessity in the form of famine had occasionally forced us into leaving home. But now a new life beckons, and reunion with a beloved son is promised. So we set out.

The common belief in this area is that a god is somehow tied to a particular locale. These Canaanites have several gods, a god of the storm, a god of the river, a god of this place or that place. Perhaps I have been infected by that belief, and in my secret heart I wondered if the God of my fathers would be left behind when I go to Egypt.

So when we set out, I planned to stop at Beersheba, the Well of the Oath,' where God had confirmed the Covenant with my father Isaac. It's the location of one of several wells my father Isaac dug years ago. It's important to have plenty of water on this trip, for one can go without food longer than without water. But it has been a place of worship for my fathers and for my family as well.

When we reached Beersheba, where my fathers have worshiped for many years, I offered sacrifices to the God of my father Isaac and his father Abraham. That night, God spoke to me in a vision, calling me by name—Jacob! Jacob!—spoken twice as one calls to a close friend.

He knew I worried about going where He was not worshiped. The Egyptians have many gods, but not the LORD, the true God. He assured me, saying:

"I am God, the God of your father. Do not be afraid to go down to Egypt, for I will make you into a great nation there.'

And then he responded to my unspoken fear when he said, *"I will go down to Egypt with you, and I will surely bring you back again. And Joseph's own hand will close your eyes." (Genesis 46:3,4)*

Years and years ago, God promised He would be with me. I sort of accepted that God is everywhere, but still I wondered, because there were times when I felt utterly alone, even deserted. But—is it possible that my God who is everywhere, will be with me—with me!— in Egypt? Is it possible that wherever I go He is with me? Even—in me?

* * *

SO THIS IS WHERE
by Betty Spence

So this is where the Lord has pitched His tent—
I am God's secret place and He is mine.
The veil of separation now is rent.
All this is where the Lord has pitched His tent.
The mountains are no more His tenement;
The wilderness no longer is His shrine.
This is where the Lord has pitched His tent—
I am God's secret place and He is mine.

* * *

God had assured me of His presence, no matter where I resided. Alive or dead, I would return to my homeland, and Joseph will be beside me when I die.

So. Egypt, here I come. Here *we* come—my God and I.   *(Jacob)*

* * *

Joseph:

My brother Judah came ahead of the rest of the family to tell me they were on the way, and to get directions to Goshen. Since there were seventy of them plus my brothers' wives, their livestock and everything they owned—well, it was a good thing Pharaoh had sent wagons for them. He had also told them not to bother with their possessions, but did you ever see anyone leave everything behind when he moves? Not likely.

When I received word they had reached Goshen, I had my chariot made ready and went to meet my father after twenty long years. We hugged and wept a long time—twenty years' worth of absence and sorrow being washed away.

I told my brothers that I would arrange a meeting with the king, and I also instructed them exactly how to respond when he asks their occupation. "Say this: 'Your servants have taken care of farm animals all our lives, just as our fathers did.' Egyptians don't like to be near shepherds, so Pharaoh will let you settle in Goshen, which is in northern Egypt and well-suited for your flocks and herds."

Well, when the king asked them, they said, "Your servants are shepherds just as our fathers were." So much for what I had advised! But anyway, when they asked to be allowed to settle in Goshen, Pharaoh approved that. He also told me, "If any of them are skilled shepherds, put them in charge of my own sheep and cattle."

After my brothers had their audience with the king, I brought my father in and presented him. When Pharaoh asked his age, Father told him, "The years of my pilgrimage are a hundred and thirty. My years have been few and difficult, and they do not equal the years of the pilgrimage of my fathers." At the end of the audience, my father blessed Pharaoh before leaving him.

I settled my family in the best part of the land as Pharaoh directed. That was the district of Rameses in the delta of the Nile. I also provided them with food during The Hunger Years. Being the one in charge of distributing food had advantages for my family. And not only my brothers; since my wife's father was the priest of On (Heliopolis), special privileges were granted to the priests. During the worst of the famine while people were selling their fields and property to Pharaoh in exchange for food, the priests received a regular allotment of food from Pharaoh and did not have to sell their land.

But as the famine years continued, the measures I had to take grew more severe. *(Joseph)*

Chapter 22. Stringent Measures

FOOD IN EXCHANGE FOR LIVESTOCK

There was no food, however, in the whole region because the famine was severe; both Egypt and Canaan wasted away because of the famine. Joseph collected all the money that was to be found in Egypt and Canaan for the grain they were buying, and he brought it to Pharaoh's palace. When the money of the people of Egypt and Canaan was gone, all Egypt came to Joseph and said, "Give us food. Why should we die before your eyes? Our money is all gone."

"Then bring your livestock," said Joseph. "I will sell you food in exchange for your livestock, since your money is gone." So they brought their livestock to Joseph, and he gave them food in exchange for their horses, their sheep and goats, their cattle and donkeys. And he brought them through that year with food in exchange for all their livestock. (Genesis 47:13-17)

Joseph:

Seeing these starving people come before me begging for food but having no money left to buy with—it can tear the heart out of you. But I was in charge of that which belonged to the king. It was not mine to give away. And the famine years stretched out ahead. What to do next?

FOOD IN EXCHANGE FOR LAND

When that year was over, they came to him the following year and said, "We cannot hide from our lord the fact that since our money is gone and our livestock belongs to you, there is nothing left for our lord except our bodies and our land. Why should we perish before your eyes—we and our land as well? Buy us and our land in exchange for food, and we with our land will be in bondage to Pharaoh. Give us seed so that we may live and not die, and that the land may not become desolate.

So Joseph bought all the land in Egypt for Pharaoh. The Egyptians, one and all, sold their fields, because the famine was too severe for them. The land became Pharaoh's, and Joseph reduced the people to servitude, from one end of Egypt to the other. (Genesis 47:18-21)

Maybe having to make these life-or-death choices would not be so hard on someone else—although I don't know anyone that hard-hearted—but I felt like a monster. I was hated yet sought out. "We with our land will be in bondage to Pharaoh," they said. And so it was. And I, Joseph, was the one who reduced the people to servitude!

What can I do to make this horrible necessity fairer, less painful? Food helps for the day or week but not for the next planting.

Unless— Yes! I can require them to double-tithe the new crop to Pharaoh. Then there will be grain coming back to the store houses, for the next year's sowing.

JOSEPH'S LAW: ONE-FIFTH
OF THE HARVEST TO PHARAOH

Joseph said to the people, "Now that I have bought you and your land today for Pharaoh, here is seed for you so you can plant the ground. But when the crop comes in, give a fifth of it to Pharaoh. The other four-fifths you may keep as seed for the fields and as food for yourselves and your households and your children.

So Joseph established it as a law concerning land in Egypt—still in force today—that a fifth of the produce belongs to Pharaoh. (Genesis 47:23-26)

Joseph's Law, they called it. That awful ruling that forced the people of Egypt to give twenty percentage of their crops to Pharaoh, right off the top. No expenses, no losses allowed. And that law carries my name. But much as I wish I was not forever tied to responsibility for that law, I am thankful I was instrumental in saving lives, thousands, maybe millions, of lives. And they were pitifully appreciative. "You have saved our lives," they said. "May we find favor in the eyes of our lord; we will be in bondage to Pharaoh."

Truly, I was sent by God ahead of my family to Egypt. *(Joseph)*

Chapter 23. Endings

JOSEPH'S SONS BLESSED

Some time later Joseph was told, "Your father is ill." So he took his two sons Manasseh and Ephraim along with him. When Jacob was told, "Your son Joseph has come to you," Israel [Jacob] rallied his strength and sat up on the bed. . . .

When Israel saw the sons of Joseph, he asked, "Who are these?" "They are the sons God has given me here," Joseph said to his father. Then Israel said, "Bring them to me so I may bless them."

Now Israel's eyes were failing because of old age, and he could hardly see. So Joseph brought his sons close to him, and his father kissed them and embraced them. Israel said to Joseph, "I never expected to see your face again, and now God has allowed me to see your children too." (Genesis 48:1,2,8-11)

Jacob:

I was nearly blind, old, sick, and almost too weak to sit up, but when these two boys were brought before me, I made the effort. Manasseh and Ephraim. Joseph gave them good old Hebrew names even though their mother is an Egyptian. I thought I would never see my son Joseph again and now here he is, standing before me with his two sons.

Sometimes the things that come out of our mouths are a surprise to ourselves. (That can be good or bad, of course. I know I've said things I wished I could take back.) But this is something God told me to say to Joseph. "Your two sons, who were born here in Egypt before I came, will be counted as my own sons. Ephraim and Manasseh will be my sons just as Reuben and Simeon are my sons. But if you have other children, they will be your own, and their land will be part of the land given to Ephraim and Manasseh."

I have no idea what difference that will make in years ahead, but I was led by God to say it. In effect, I was adopting those boys, counting them into my family of sons. They will take the place of Reuben who had forfeited his first-son status by sleeping with Bilhah my concubine, and also the place of their father Joseph who has no need of any inheritance from me.

Then Joseph brought the boys near. Look, I'm a grandfather, so I do what loving grandfathers do. I just had to put my arms around them and kiss them. Maybe Joseph thought they were too heavy for me, for he moved them off my lap. He knew I intended to bless them, so he arranged them by placing Ephraim on his right and Manasseh on his left, which made Ephraim on my left side and Manasseh on my right. That would be customary: the right side for the oldest. But, without my planning it or even knowing why, I crossed my arms and put my right hand on the younger boy, Ephraim.

First I blessed Joseph and the boys, saying:

"May the God before whom my fathers Abraham and Isaac walked faithfully,
the God who has been my shepherd all my life to this day,
the Angel who has delivered me from all harm--may he bless these boys.
May they be called by my name and the names of my fathers Abraham and Isaac,
and may they increase greatly on the earth. (Genesis 48:15,16)*

Joseph thought I had made a mistake in putting my right hand on the younger boy, so he tried to move my hand. "That's wrong, Father. Manasseh is the firstborn."

I said, "I know, my son. I know. Manasseh will be great and have many descendants. But his younger brother will be greater and his descendants will be enough to make a nation."

Then I blessed both boys, saying:

In your name will Israel pronounce this blessing:
'May God make you like Ephraim and Manasseh.'"

I don't understand what meaning that has or will have; I am just the one through whom God chose to prophecy.

I had a special word for Joseph too: "God will take you back to the land of your fathers. I am giving you something I didn't give the others. You will have the land of Shechem that I took from the Amorites with my sword and my bow."

And now this old warrior feels his last battle is approaching. I must call all my sons together to hear what God has shown me for their futures.   *(Jacob)*

* * *

JACOB BLESSES AND PROPHESIES

Judah:

Before Father died, he called us all together and prophesied over us. Some things he said were most puzzling; mine in particular.

One thing Father said about me sounded like one of those dreams Joseph had, the one that angered all of us, even Father and Mother. My prophecy said that my brothers will praise me and bow down to me. I hope my brothers don't take my prophecy to heart and turn against me, like we did to Joseph. Maybe we've grown up a bit by now. I hope so.

But the part that really puzzled me was:

The scepter will not depart from Judah, nor the ruler's staff from between his feet, until he to whom it belongs shall come and the obedience of the nations shall be his. (Genesis 49:10)

It sounds like a king or kings may be among my descendants. It reminded me of the LORD's covenant with Abraham and Isaac, that kings would come from his line. But I'm a shepherd. Really now, whoever heard of a shepherd becoming a king?   *(Judah)*

* * *

Jacob lived in Egypt seventeen years, and the years of his life were a hundred and forty-seven. When the time drew near for Israel to die, he called for his son Joseph and said to him, "Do not bury me in Egypt, but when I rest with my fathers, carry me out of Egypt and bury me where they are buried."
"I will do as you say," he said.   (Genesis 47:28-30)

* * *

JACOB'S FUNERAL PROCESSION

Judah:

When Father died, they embalmed his body (that took forty days) and we held a mourning period for seventy days altogether. Then we all joined into a huge procession to take his body back to the family burial cave.

When I say "huge" procession, I'm not exaggerating. Because Joseph is such a great man in Egypt (vizier of the Pharaoh), he was accompanied by all the king's officials—not only the dignitaries of Pharaoh's court but of all Egypt—plus all the members of Joseph's household and of his brothers' households (except the nursing mothers and the little ones), and many chariots and horsemen.

When we came to the threshing floor of Atad near the Jordan, we stopped for a seven-day period of mourning. And, as you know, we don't mourn quietly. When the Canaanites who lived in that area saw us (and heard us), they said, "The Egyptians are holding a solemn ceremony of mourning." In fact, after that, they renamed the place Abel Mizraim which means "Sorrow of the Egyptians." It's no surprise we brothers were also taken for Egyptians. By that time we mostly wore Egyptian dress when we weren't working in the fields.

Years before, Father had told Joseph he wanted to be taken back to Canaan and be laid in the cave with his fathers. So we did as he said, and carried Father's body to the cave our great-grandfather Abraham had bought for a family burial place. There we laid our father beside our ancestors Abraham and Sarah, Isaac and Rebekah, and my own mother Leah.

BROTHERS FEAR

But when we got back to Egypt, we began to worry. Maybe Joseph really hadn't forgiven us, and had just held back while Father was alive. What if he decides to pay us back for what we did to him?

So we sent him the following message:

"Your father left these instructions before he died. This is what you are to say to Joseph: 'I ask you to forgive your brothers the sins and the wrongs they committed in treating you so badly.' Now please forgive the sins of the servants of the God of your father.'"   *(Genesis 50:16,17)*

Of course Father had never told us this, but seeing how important Joseph was in Egypt, quite frankly, we were afraid. Then we all went to Joseph, threw ourselves down before him, and said, "We are your slaves." *(Judah)*

Joseph:

Ah, these brothers of mine! They break my heart! How could they not believe that I had truly forgiven them? Surely, in the last seventeen years, I had shown them my forgiveness by the way I provided both food and the best land for them.

But I reassured them:

Don't be afraid. Am I in the place of God? You intended to harm me, but God intended it for good to accomplish what is now being done, the saving of many lives. So then, don't be afraid. I will provide for you and your children."
(Genesis 50:16-21)

How many times do I have to tell them? You meant to harm me, but God turned your evil into good! God intended it for good! *(Joseph)*

* * *

DEATH OF JOSEPH

Joseph stayed in Egypt, along with all his father's family. He lived a hundred and ten years and saw the third generation of Ephraim's children. Also the children of Makir son of Manasseh were placed at birth on Joseph's knees. Then Joseph said to his brothers, "I am about to die. But God will surely come to your aid and take you up out of this land to the land he promised on oath to Abraham, Isaac, and Jacob.

He made them swear an oath that when they leave Egypt, they will take his bones with them.

Joseph died at the age of a hundred and ten years. And after they embalmed him, he was placed in a coffin in Egypt. *(Genesis 50:22-26)*

* * *

This is the end of Genesis, the end of the beginning.

BUT . . . .

GROUNDWORK LAID FOR EXODUS

Now Joseph and all his brothers and all that generation died, but the Israelites were exceedingly fruitful; they multiplied greatly, increased in numbers and became so numerous that the land was filled with them. Then a new king, to whom Joseph meant nothing, came to power in Egypt. (Exodus 1:6-8)

The Israelite people lived in Egypt for 430 years. At the end of the 430 years, to the very day, all the LORD's divisions left Egypt. (Exodus 12:40,41)

Moses took the bones of Joseph with him because Joseph had made the Israelites swear an oath. He had said, "God will surely come to your aid, and then you must carry my bones up with you from this place." (Exodus 13:19)

* * *

**Exodus: the beginning of a new nation
throwing off the chains of slavery
striking out into the unknown
following Moses, a descendant of Levi
learning about Yahweh, the LORD God of their
fathers.
A new adventure:
in step —with God!**

THE END – YES

BUT ALSO

A NEW BEGINNING

65844024R00077

Made in the USA
Lexington, KY
26 July 2017